THE RENAISSANCE REWIRED

GOVERNING IN THE AGE OF AI AND COMPLEXITY

ROBERT H. HACKER

innovativeink
PUBLISHING
A Division of Kendall Hunt

Cover images Shutterstock.com

innovativeink PUBLISHING
A Division of Kendall Hunt

www.innovativeinkpublishing.com
Send all inquiries to:
4050 Westmark Drive
Dubuque, IA 52004-1840

Print ISBN: 979-8-3851-8162-9
Ebook ISBN: 979-8-3851-8163-6

Published in the United States of America

Contents

Preface

> "You are not here merely to make a living. You are here in order to enable the world to live more amply, with greater vision, with a finer spirit of hope and achievement. You are here to enrich the world, and you impoverish yourself if you forget the errand."
>
> —Woodrow Wilson

THE PROBLEM

History is at perhaps the most dramatic inflection point since the Renaissance and the intellectual contributions of da Vinci, Newton, Descartes, and many others. Today I believe we are in the Second Renaissance, a period to be shaped by artificial intelligence and remarkable advances in science, engineering, and medicine. However, these advances will add complexity and increase uncertainty to levels we have not managed before. Add in the approaching environmental deadlines, the continuing disagreements between the United States and China and the inability of the United States to define and plot a new strategy and you have what the author Sebastian Junger might call a "perfect storm."

Such a future should be managed by a framework of research—innovation—entrepreneurship, and supported by government funding, basic research by academics and corporate commercialization to produce economic and social benefit at scale. Quantitative methods will support much of this progress, but qualitative thinking will shape the problem(s) to be solved and be the deciding factor to evaluate the outcomes. To support such a qualitative approach, I introduce three concepts or tools:

1. Complex adaptive systems
2. Emergent strategy
3. Systems thinking.

Complex adaptive systems (CAS) is a robust approach to understand natural and manmade systems and their interactions. Based on CAS, emergent strategy presents a component approach where different organizations contribute their specific expertise and funding to solve a bigger problem. Systems thinking provides the holistic approach to consider the environment, all the stakeholders, and the desired outcomes.

Such an approach would serve to update or modernize our model of government, which has seen few changes from its hierarchical top-down operating model since the 1700s. In fact, the two most dramatic advances in government in the United States—equal rights and women's liberation—were citizen led, bottom-up, self-organized movements consistent with CAS principles. *Updating, redefining, and reorganizing the U.S. federal government to succeed in this complex environment is a major objective of this book.*

BACKGROUND

My career has included extensive work with federal governments worldwide, with intertwined recurring themes of technology, entrepreneurship, and education. Early on, I worked for Chase Manhattan Bank lending to Latin American governments, followed by an economic analysis of mining for the Peru government and technology licensing and strategy work in Japan. I arranged licenses for e-commerce and Japan's first ISP, which is still the largest in the country. Following time in Japan, I moved on to Indonesia. I built a US$1 billion publicly traded retail company utilizing advanced data management across ten time zones. After returning to the United States in 2000, I led a Miami telephone company's shift toward data services.

My deepest insights into government came through two academic projects. At the MIT One Laptop per Child (OLPC) project, I sold approximately one million laptops to ten governments worldwide, observing firsthand how government officials' priorities often favor self-interest over education. I raised US$17M in grants and taught social entrepreneurship at MIT Sloan (IAP) for seven years, believing such an approach to entrepreneurship offers a viable alternative to government solutions for social problems.

Since 2016, I have served as the Director of StartUP FIU at the state university, Florida International University (FIU). Since 2018, I have focused on commercializing faculty research through federal agency grants, corporate sponsored research, and licensing. Working with the National Science Foundation (NSF) and Department of Energy has shown me federal government at its highest level of strategic vision and excellence. *I believe educational reform is critical to support a more modern, redesigned federal government.* My proposal here to reshape modern education draws on experiences at OLPC, MIT, and FIU over the past eighteen years.

This volume follows my first book, "The Second Renaissance: AI is Transforming Science, Technology and Entrepreneurship," and may be followed by a third book, "The Second Renaissance: Reshaping the Modern Corporation." We begin to explore the modern corporation in Chapter 15 with a discussion of the modern ecosystem and the new role for corporates.

ACKNOWLEDGMENTS

I am enormously grateful to my FIU colleague Emily Gresham for her time, review, and support of this book and all my writing. I also want to thank all my Honors College students at FIU for their patience as my thinking evolved in their classes. I thank Honors College Dean JC Espinosa who for ten years has supported the evolution of my course materials and curriculum.

I wish to highlight the patience and support from Angela Lampe at my publisher Kendall Hunt. Thank you.

I also wish to thank my wife Hortensia who suggested I go to business school, encouraged me to start my first business and has always been the adviser and supporter for my four or five different careers and my writing.

HACKER NATION

Introduction

> "No one can know the future. It seems to me the difficulty of knowing the future does not absolve the teacher from seriously trying to help the student to be ready for it when it comes."
>
> —Richard W. Hamming, The Art of Doing Science and Engineering

In an era of unprecedented global complexity and uncertainty, humanity finds itself at a critical crossroads. This convergence and the intricate interplay between natural and artificial systems has created a world that defies simple solutions. As we grapple with challenges that span environmental, social, and technological domains, it becomes increasingly clear that our traditional approaches to problem-solving became outdated at the start of the Fourth Industrial Revolution, what I call the Knowledge Revolution. In 2016, the World Economic Forum proclaimed the Fourth Industrial Revolution and the commercial readiness of artificial intelligence (AI) and machine learning (ML). The Stanford Institute for Human-Centered AI might have claimed this revolution started as early as 2009 with advances in deep-learning algorithms. By late 2023, OpenAI claimed 100 million active users for its latest AI model. This success galvanized a reportedly two million developers, entrepreneurs, and venture capitalists (VCs) to initiate commercial efforts using AI.[1]

This scale and speed of technological adoption is unprecedented, which prompts me to call it the Second Renaissance. Drawing comparisons, the first Renaissance produced major contributions in mathematics, science, and later in the writings on democratic government by Rousseau and Montesquieu. Advances in mathematical notation, logarithms, and analytical geometry are examples of the advances in mathematics, and advances in science included the development of the scientific method, initial understanding of anatomy, and exploration of planetary motion. *The Second Renaissance is being led by AI/ML, a toolset that I think will prove to be comparable to the contribution of mathematics!* Modern science uses the building blocks of molecules, atoms, and elementary particles out of which all matter is made; cells, proteins, and genes make life possible; these datasets are so perfectly suited for the pattern recognition and quantitative methods of AI/ML.

Much less publicized but equally important, the magnitude of the change from AI/ML prompts an accompanying need to update our social systems and government for this new technology. To fully realize these benefits we need to design, build and constantly update the chips, data, algorithms and energy technology to support this infrastructure. The concomitant need is the necessary update to public education to prepare youth to produce the full benefits from this new technology for mankind.

This book delves into the heart of this dilemma, exploring the urgent need for counterbalancing conceptual innovation in our rapidly evolving technology-driven world. Drawing inspiration from Jean Piaget's prescient observation that "Only education is capable of saving our societies from possible collapse," we embark on a journey to reimagine the fundamental structures that shape our society.

At the core of our exploration lies the concept of CAS, a framework that offers profound insights into the behavior of markets, natural ecosystems,

1. https://techcrunch.com/2023/11/06/openais-chatgpt-now-has-100-million-weekly-active-users/

and civil society. Yet, as we will discover, two crucial pillars of our world—government and education—remain rooted in outdated, linear paradigms. This misalignment forms the crux of our inability to effectively address the multifaceted challenges of the twenty-first century. Conceptual innovation, more than new technology, will be required to redefine the future.

Through a comprehensive analysis, this book charts a path forward. *We examine how conceptual innovation, far more transformative than mere technological advancement, can reshape our approach to governance, education, and problem-solving across all sectors.* From reimagining government as an adaptive, experimental entity to revolutionizing sociocultural systems in a complex, AI-driven world, we explore the much-needed new strategies for institutional evolution in healthcare, the environment, and energy. Henry Mintzberg's work and systems thinking help us to reach more comprehensive, holistic understanding.

The choices we make today may shape the trajectory and future of human civilization. *This book serves as both a wake-up call and a roadmap, challenging readers and leaders to embrace a new paradigm of thinking and action.* The book is an invitation to participate in the most crucial task of our time: the reinvention of democratic government. Therein lies the need for conceptual innovation!

THE OBJECTIVES

This book has four primary objectives:

1. To prepare readers for a future transformed by artificial intelligence, biotechnology, sensor networks, and robotics.
2. To explain how we need to pay critical attention to conceptual innovation and not be swept along just by technological advances.
3. To offer an innovative redefinition of government and related strategy, applying the theory of CAS to governance.

4. To reshape modern education as an integral part of my new formulation for government.

Each of these objectives is also a field for future research. For example:

1. Which technologies will be spun out of the AI/ML technology to shape the future? Will it be biopharma, materials science, defense tech, or another field?
2. What would be required for a significant update to be defined and implemented for the U.S. federal government?
3. Can the U.S. government be modernized as a CAS or will it increasingly become a more dysfunctional top-down hierarchy?

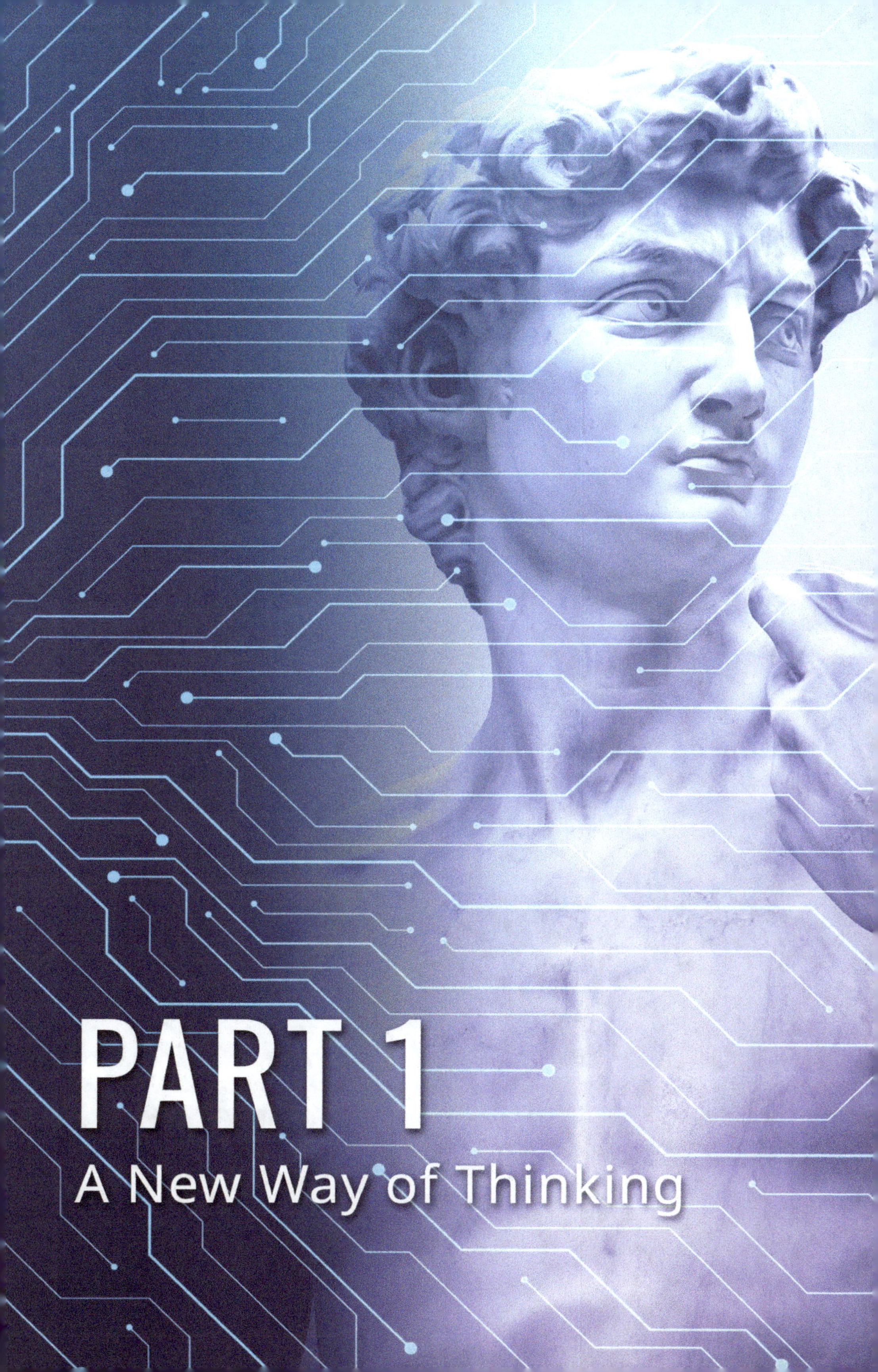

PART 1

A New Way of Thinking

1

Creativity and Conceptual Innovation

"Art is but one way of contacting that deeper reality. Science is another, with its revelations of truths so beyond sight that they seem inconceivable, from the billions of neutrinos passing through your body this very second to the hummingbird's flight to the quantum bewilderment of the subatomic world."

—Maria Popova. Marginalian

THE PROBLEM

Today creativity, invention and innovation are frequently cited to explain entrepreneurship and the related social benefits. However, in my experience, most people cannot define nor explain these concepts. Instead, we almost blindly embrace AI-driven entrepreneurship and economic development at breakneck speed fueled by record amounts of available capital. I am not so concerned by the ethical issues and bad actors, which I think are just the growing pains of this novel and adaptable AI technology. I am more concerned that the talent may be overlooking the opportunities based on qualitative analysis, such as the social imperatives for environmental and social advances, in favor of a tunnel vision focus on quantitative analysis for solutions. To better understand both the social and economic opportunities, I will begin by first presenting the Krebs Creativity Cycle (KCC)[1] to further explain conceptual innovation.

THE ABSTRACT, CONCEPTUAL INNOVATION

In 2016, MIT Media Lab professor Neri Oxman wrote a fascinating article, "Age of Entanglement,"[2] to explore the creative domains of Art, Science, Engineering, and Design. The reader should appreciate that these four domains explain all forms of creativity. Oxman hoped to show "that knowledge can no longer be ascribed to, or produced within, disciplinary boundaries, but is entirely entangled." In Media Lab speak, this concept is called antidisciplinary, but I will use the more traditional multidisciplinary, interdisciplinary, or transdisciplinary, as appropriate, in this book.[3]

As shown below, we can think of the KCC as a circle, with distinct boundaries between the four domains. Art takes our perceptions and converts them to tangible through painting, drawing, music, writing, and now all of these in digital formats. Driven by curiosity about what we perceive, science takes data and information and creates knowledge. Throughout history, the intersection of art and science has led to groundbreaking discoveries and masterpieces. Leonardo da Vinci's anatomical drawings might be the most frequently cited example, but James Audubon's naturalist drawings of North American birds and Santiago Ramon y Cajal's neuroscience sketches are other noteworthy examples.

Einstein explained the similarity between art and science.

> The most beautiful experience we can have is the mysterious. It is the fundamental emotion which stands at the cradle of true art and true science.

1. https://jods.mitpress.mit.edu/pub/ageofentanglement/release/1
2. https://jods.mitpress.mit.edu/pub/ageofentanglement/release/1
3. I do not see the difference between antidisciplinary and transdisciplinary, the combination of multiple fields into a new field of study. Maybe Oxman has better marketing skills than me.

Schopenhauer confirms Einstein.

> Art takes the emotions and makes them tangible.

These geniuses show us that both art and science take the abstract and make them tangible. And at the border between science and art, we have mathematics, which seeks to validate the abstract. The Russian mathematician Nikolay Lobachevsky explains it well, "There is no branch of mathematics, however abstract, which may not someday be applied to phenomena of the real world." Mathematics takes information in the many formats of experimental observation and identifies patterns and understanding (mathematical insight). The combination of pattern recognition and probability is perhaps the simplest way to explain how humans learn and, interestingly, the simplest way to explain AI. You should no longer be surprised by the constant stream of new uses of AI in art and science.

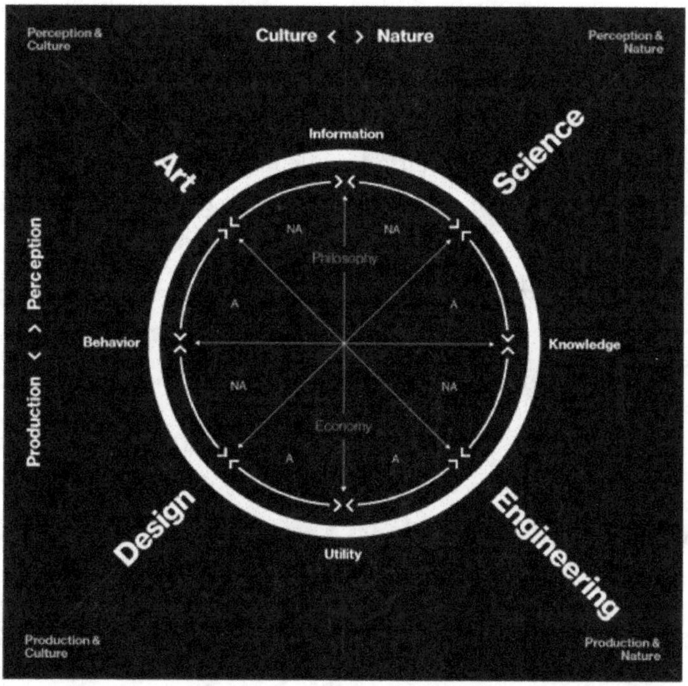

FIGURE 1.

I think of the top half of the KCC as the "abstract," concepts formed by extracting from the data (sensory inputs) and information (selected data). For simplicity and ease of understanding, I will use "conceptual" rather than abstract. *Innovation in art and science will be referred to as "conceptual innovation."* And, if you think about it, all transformative and innovative thinking begins in the arts and sciences. Art converts human, cultural behavior and observation into the data and information that prompts the holistic philosophical and scientific inquiry. To paraphrase Herbert Simon, "If science is to encompass these objects and phenomena in which human purpose as well as natural law are embodied, it must have means for relating these two disparate components."[4] These means I call conceptual innovation. We need abstract models to tackle complex problems.

Further explanation might make Simon's point and my concept of conceptual innovation clearer. At the most basic level, humans take in data across the boundaries of the five human senses. These "predictions" advance upward through a nested hierarchy in the brain where higher levels adjust for discrepancies in the data based on past experience. Reaching the highest levels of "certainty," this data is then qualified as information. The scientist would apply the scientific method to determine that this information is sufficiently certain, useful, and applicable to be deemed knowledge. Alternatively, the artist shares their sensory perceptions as information in the form of art. Really, the only difference between the scientist and the artist is the form of the final output. For all humans, the cognitive processes at the most basic level use pattern recognition and the determination of probabilities to develop information and knowledge.

TECHNOLOGICAL INNOVATION

In the bottom half of the KCC, we have engineering and design. Engineering takes science and gives it tangible purpose. Design takes engineering in the form of technology and gives it utility. To paraphrase Herbert Simon again,

4. Simon, H. *The Sciences of the Artificial.*

design is tangible problem-solving for a user. Since 1997, the National Science Foundation (NSF) has been trying to move scientific research beyond "science for science's sake" to focus science on problem-solving for a user, as Simon described. NASA has been trying to achieve this objective since the Apollo project began in 1961. I have worked with over 70 scientific and engineering researchers at FIU. I recommend that if one is doing research, then one should begin their research first by identifying the problem to be solved and then developing an explicit innovative solution to the problem.

The bottom half of the KCC diagram, engineering and design, I combine in the term "technological innovation." "Technological" innovation has been well defined since the time of the economist Joseph Schumpeter. To paraphrase Schumpeter, innovation is invention commercialized. "This principle underscores the importance as both a challenge and an opportunity of the continual replacement, renewal and reinvention of socioeconomic, technological and political institutions, practices, and infra-structures."[5]

Schumpeter's perspective highlights that innovation is not merely about creating new ideas or technologies (invention) but about successfully applying those ideas in ways that generate value through commercialization. An example illustrates the point. Google did not invent the Internet or the search function, but they revolutionized both incredibly useful technologies through their success in commercializing Google search. If the federal government would demonstrate the willingness to change, as a first customer, it could validate many technologies as commercially ready.

Herbert Simon did much work to define "design" and lay the foundation for the ever-popular design thinking. For Simon, design was the selection from the possible solutions (the decision-making) to solve a problem for the identified user or customer. Simon combined technology (the result of the engineering) and utility (the satisfaction of the human need) to set the stage for best practices in design beginning in the 1960s.

5. https://www.sciencedirect.com/science/article/pii/S0166497205000738#fn4

SOME TOOLS

In the 1960s, NASA developed a scale of Technical Readiness Levels (TRL) from 1 to 9 to better manage the Apollo Project to put a man on the moon. Schumpeter's innovation would be TRL 7 and invention would be TRL 6 or what the entrepreneurs call MVP (minimum viable product). NASA defined TRL 6 as "a system or subsystem model validated in a relevant environment." TRL 7 is "a system prototype demonstrated in an operational environment."[6] "Operational" I translate into "saleable," usable by customers.

Clayton Christensen at Harvard Business School (HBS) advanced our understanding of innovation by coining the term "disruptive innovation." Christensen defined disruptive innovation as:

> Disruptive innovation describes a process by which a product or service powered by a technology enabler initially takes root in simple applications at the low end of a market—typically by being less expensive and more accessible—and then relentlessly moves upmarket, eventually displacing established competitors.[7]

The popularity of Christensen and the increasing capital allocated to venture capital investment in startups has prompted almost everyone to define innovation as technological. BCG, McKinsey, and the major universities all define it this way. In the vernacular, "innovation" may have some other undefined meaning, but today innovation is narrowly defined as technological.

As the National Institute of Health (NIH) states it, "given its critical importance to our success, it is surprising that our understanding of innovation in humans, including its evolutionary foundations, developmental trajectory, and contextual facilitators, is still in its infancy."[8] This book introduc-

6. https://www.sciencedirect.com/topics/engineering/technology-readiness-level#:~:text=Level%20 1:%20Basic%20principles%20observed,science/article/pii/S1364032118300431
7. https://sloanreview.mit.edu/article/an-interview-with-clayton-m-christensen/
8. https://pmc.ncbi.nlm.nih.gov/articles/PMC5053256/

es, defines, and explains conceptual innovation, which I will do in the next chapter. The basic premise of my argument is that we have become very successful in the development of technological innovation, particularly since information, and more specifically digital information, became the modern value creator. However, I am afraid that we might get lazy, focus on technological innovation, and lose sight of the urgent need for more conceptual innovation in the arts and sciences. *The problems today are complex, multidisciplinary,*[9] *and based in a world with unprecedented uncertainty. Such challenges require a return to the fundamentals of knowledge—to art and science*—and the reexamination of some our most traditional concepts and organizations, such as federal government and education.

REVOLUTIONARY INNOVATION

Another point about innovation needs explanation—the distinction between incremental and revolutionary innovation. Incremental innovation is the iterative process of small steps to optimize an existing offering. I see it more as a management process like productivity and efficiency improvement and not as innovation. The IBM Institute for Business Value finds that "over the next three years, 85% of executives say that AI will enable business model innovation."[10] This is an example of incremental innovation. Revolutionary innovation is the radical, groundbreaking development that changes the frontiers of science, engineering, or medicine and creates new opportunity. The first medical therapies, electricity, and the computer were all new innovations created by redefining the boundaries of knowledge. Hereafter, when I use "innovation," I refer only to the "revolutionary."

Earlier I stated that a researcher should identify the problem first and then pursue an innovative solution. Now we know that this innovation should be revolutionary and not the incremental innovations that do not create

9. Note: Interdisciplinary—an approach whereby multiple disciplines are integrated from the start (as opposed to multidisciplinary where the research from different fields is combined at the conclusion).
10. https://www.ibm.com/thought-leadership/institute-business-value/en-us/report/business-trends-2025

significant value for the customer. The widespread availability of AI/ML, and the tools to manipulate large amounts of data and other digital information, creates the value for a business or consumer. Michael Porter at HBS proposed that competitive advantage provided the basis to capture value and that a business model based on focus, differentiation, or lowest cost was the most effective way to create and preserve value for the customer. For Porter, focus was the singular attention to understanding the social, biological, and emotional needs of one customer segment in a market. Differentiation was the use of revolutionary innovation to better serve the customer and low cost while self-explanatory requires constant attention. Cadillac's success with female drivers exemplifies focus. Medtronic's original pacemaker was an example of differentiation through revolutionary innovation. Walmart is a legendary example of a low-cost strategy.

2

Conceptual Innovation: The Unseen Force of Change

> "We live in a time where all current systems of human thought from physics to politics are dominated by a set of underlying assumptions that are mostly outdated and no longer work in a very different world that is more interdependent and connected than ever before in human history."[1]
>
> —Fritjof Capra

If we look at the history of man, evolution provided the ability to survive and reproduce. Evolution also provided the ability to trust and collaborate. This was the foundation for all other human behavior to be learned. Two of the most significant early developments were:

1. the ability of man to stand on two feet, and
2. the ability to communicate through voice or early language.

Standing on two feet changed the risk horizon because a standing man could see farther. Such a standing man had a better chance to avoid the predators and find more game for dinner. Such successes prompted a need

1. Capra F., and P. L. Luisi, *The Systems View of Life: A Unifying Vision* (Cambridge, England: Cambridge University Press).

for verbal communication to share the information with other hunters now hunting farther apart. To this point I am just documenting evolution, survival of the fittest, and the early days of speech and collaboration. However, these advantages prompted man to be more purposeful and to advance language skills and develop languages, develop drawing and art, music, and eventually writing, probably in that order. What one realizes is that all of these "arts" were simply advances in communication and collaboration initially. These advances provided increasingly sophisticated means for humans to share their abstractions from perception, emotions, and thought. What one can easily see is that from a starting point in primitive speech, man developed significant conceptual innovations—art, music, and writing—that were tangible and have shaped human history for thousands of years.

Throughout this book I make a distinction between data, information, and knowledge. Data is the raw perception. Information is the data selected from one's perception (pattern recognition) and knowledge unifies our understanding of reality. It is in this unification of understanding that we find the new models and boundaries of a discipline, showcase a new methodology, and/or present the conceptual innovations. Modern best practices dictate that each conceptual innovation proposes a solution to a problem for a particular user group (Porter's "focus").

Some might say these developments in the arts are technological innovations, but I would point out that there was no significant use of engineering nor design. Art was a new means to transfer information. For example, drawing on the cave walls showed the animals in the vicinity. The different animal drawings reinforced the use of pattern recognition as the means to identify the different animals. Music served multiple purposes—to show emotion, to entertain, and to foster group collaboration through nonthreatening dancing and singing. When song was added, it encouraged people to memorize the spoken word. As Gutenberg dramatically demonstrated with the invention of the printing press a few thousand years later, writing was the most efficient, economical way to share data, information, and knowledge … until the digital era and the Internet. These new arts solved a problem for a user group, a very large user group found around the world in almost every population. These arts communicated information derived from the abstraction of sensory data in the increasingly sophisticated ways that made the development of science possible.

Today science includes three branches:

1. Natural sciences
2. Social sciences
3. Formal sciences.

Natural sciences include physics, chemistry, biology, and the earth sciences. Social sciences include psychology, sociology, economics, political science, and anthropology. Formal sciences include mathematics, statistics, logic, and theoretical computer science.

Outstanding examples of conceptual innovation in science are:

- The transformative physics of Max Planck, Albert Einstein, and others that replaced what we now call Newton's classical physics
- Watson and Crick's discovery of DNA
- Ben Franklin's discovery of electricity.

Most of the advances in the twentieth and twenty-first centuries have come from scientific investigation, what some call scientific "discovery." I prefer to call it conceptual innovation to reinforce the abstract nature of science and that innovation sets a standard for the science as "revolutionary" or boundary redefining. I think the similarities between science and art have been lost over the centuries and their common definition as conceptual innovation helps preserve the essence of both domains.

Since the time of the Greeks, science has been a "synthetic visualization" of abstract concepts. For example, most of physics is not observable but we have developed the mathematics to document statistical mechanics, quantum physics, and entropy to name a few revolutionary, frontier redefining examples. James Gleick, referring to Isaac Newton's view, described mathematics as a "symbolic translation."[2] Science has now advanced through four phases:

1. Experimentation
2. Theory
3. Modeling and simulation
4. Artificial Intelligence (AI).

When we look at the modern problems of the environment and social issues, even with the advances in applied AI, I am still concerned about progress. I think we have the interdisciplinary knowledge in biology, chemistry, and geological sciences required to solve the problems. What we lack to solve the environmental and social problems is the concerted behavioral modification to make the sacrifices and changes in lifestyle.

In 2014, NSF requested a study of "advanced computing" in science and engineering from the National Academies of Sciences, Engineering, and Medicine (NASEM). The use of the term "advanced computing," the combination of both compute and data-intensive capabilities, not only set the stage for the final report in 2016 but also redefined modern science. The study demonstrated that data-intensive computing had advanced to become the fourth principle of science. This NSF study put the scientific community on notice that these advances in computing were critical for the technological leadership and competitiveness of the United States. The NSF wanted to ensure that the United States had the resources, infrastructure, and access to these emerging technologies. The intellectual power of the research community combined with AI/ML was needed to undertake the anticipated technological, economic, social, environmental, and national security challenges. The World Economic Forum's announcement the same year of the "Fourth Industrial Revolution" popularized "artificial intelligence as the basis for the next round of scientific and technological advances."[3]

2. Gleick, James. 2003. *Isaac Newton*. Pantheon Books.
3. Hacker, R. H., *The Second Renaissance: AI Is Transforming Science, Technology and Entrepreneurship*.

When we look at the modern problems of the environment and social issues, even with the advances in applied AI, I am still concerned about progress. In the case of the environment, I think we have the interdisciplinary knowledge in biology, chemistry, and geological sciences required to solve the problems. What we lack to solve the environmental and social problems is the concerted behavioral modification to make the sacrifices and changes in life style. We also lack today the will to coordinate this behavior at scale on an appropriate schedule, a failing that I attribute to government. More funding for social entrepreneurship might even demonstrate to the multinationals the opportunities of the environmental problems, which would be another means to achieve scale. This coordination is further complicated because environmental problems are steeped in both natural and manmade systems. None of our description of science above included a transdisciplinary study of science, systems thinking, and social issues.

Walter Buckley coined the term "complex adaptive systems" in 1968 to bring attention to the closed system that was "endemic" to the social problems of the times and complexity science was birthed.[4] In 1984, the Santa Fe Institute (SFI) was organized to study the fundamental principles of CAS and complexity science began to draw attention. In the next, chapter I explain the little-known science of complexity science and CAS.

4. Buckley, W. 1968. "Society as a Complex Adaptive System."

3

Complex Adaptive Systems: Nature's Blueprint for Resilience

"The good news is that, as Leibniz suggested, we appear to live in the best of all possible worlds, where the computable functions make life predictable enough to be survivable, while the noncomputable functions make life (and mathematical truth) unpredictable enough to remain interesting, no matter how far computers continue to advance."[1,2]

COMPLEX ADAPTIVE SYSTEMS

It took from the seventeenth century and Leibniz's profound insight until 1968 and Walter Buckley, a social scientist, to propose the science of CAS and complexity science. You may wonder why it took so long for this new science, this transformative, boundary-changing conceptual innovation, to appear. Why did it take so long to realize that natural and manmade systems are an integral whole, what we call a CAS or maybe now an ecosystem. Why did it take a social scientist?

1. George Dyson, *Turing's Cathedral.*

2. Gottfried Leibniz was a 17th-century German polymath renowned for his work in philosophy, mathematics (calculus), and science.

Perhaps we were distracted by issues in physics such as string theory or perhaps we needed better tools to understand uncertainty and complexity. Chaos theory was responsive to the need to better understand uncertainty and nonlinear systems and the work of Edward Lorenz and Benoit Mandelbrot in the 1960s advanced Poincare's original work on nonlinear systems. The focus on nonlinear systems also supported Jay Forrester's work at MIT in the 1960s that birthed systems thinking. Systems thinking emphasizes a holistic approach to understand the agents, elements, and environment of a boundary-defined system. Bringing together nonlinear systems, chaos theory, and systems thinking as an integrated whole was perhaps the foundation for CAS. Fritjof Capra, physicist and author of "The Systems View of Life," explains it well:

> Nonlinear dynamics, then, represents a qualitative rather than a quantitative approach to complexity and thus embodies the shift of perspective that is characteristic of systems thinking—from objects to relationships, from measuring to mapping, from quantity to quality.[3]

There are many definitions of CAS. I like W. Bryan Arthur's definition. He is a retired Stanford economics professor and a cofounder of SFI, perhaps the leading CAS research center in the world. He defines (2015) a CAS with the following fundamental characteristics.[4]

1. Emergence—Unexpected outcomes arise that are not explainable or predictable, e.g., phase transitions
2. Hierarchical—Nested [sub]systems are an integral part of a larger system with no dictated instruction from outside the system
3. Nonlinear—Agents have random or chaotic behavior (unpredictable and uncertain)
4. Adaptive—Agents learn or evolve based on information or the related feedback
5. Self-organizing—Agents and [sub]systems are autonomous to achieve purpose

3. Fritjof Capra and Pier Luigi Luisi, *The Systems View of Life.*
4. Hacker, R. H. *The Second Renaissance: AI Is Transforming Science, Technology and Entrepreneurship.*

(I reorder the fundamentals of complexity using the mnemonic "SHANE.")

CAS APPLIED

To summarize and explain the interaction of these features, we focus on emergence, "the phenomenon where novel and coherent structures, patterns, and properties arise from the interactions of the system's parts [components]."[5] Emergence takes place through nonlinear interactions between components, made possible by self-organizing, networked connectivity that facilitates various forms of exchange and interaction, including information and energy transfer. "In most complex adaptive systems, building blocks [components] at one level of complexity are combined to get building blocks for structures at a higher level of complexity. This layered use of building blocks [hierarchy] can be compared to the combination of nucleons to get atoms, which in turn are combined to get molecules, and so on. This plausible, experience-based nature of layered structures formed of tested building blocks again holds whether we are talking of evolution, innovation, or mathematical proofs."[6] Even human cognitive process uses a layered, nested hierarchy of processing systems to validate information as knowledge. A nested hierarchy is made possible by the ever-pervasive network, which serves as the means for interaction between connected processing agents in all living things. Larger networks produce higher-quality results and enhance survival. As unpredictable mutations change the performance characteristics of a networked agent, a new distinctive emergent functionality may be produced. Lesser-quality results lead to extinction of the species. This network-based emergence is how we evolved from slime molds to humans and probably why it took four billion years. To restate, CAS were developed from four billion years of evolution in natural systems, then adopted by man and then recognized as science beginning only in the 1960s. These four billion years tested and refined a versatile systems methodology built on networks devoted to survival in almost all possible

5. https://www.frontiersin.org/journals/sociology/articles/10.3389/fsoc.2022.1102815/full#B20
6. John H. Holland, *Signals and Boundaries.*

environments. If you like, we could say that we tested the computational model for 4+ billion years.

Today, complexity science is used in biology and all the branches of environmental science, the social sciences of economics, political science and sociology, urban studies, computer science, power systems, neuroscience, and psychology. CAS study is shaped by an interdisciplinary focus and computational methods, such as:

- Agent-based Modeling (ABM)—simulating agents to show emergent system-level behavior
- Scaling Laws—shows how system features change with scale
- Network Analysis—analyzing the components, topology, and information flow of systems
- Machine Learning—using the latest advances in information theory and algorithms to analyze complex data sets to understand emergent behavior.

I think CAS is the perfect tool to understand the complexity and uncertainty of the modern world. CAS is also the near-perfect model for the increasingly apparent information-centric model for value creation and economic development. To quote David Krakauer, the President of SFI, "The complex domain encompasses the world of self-organizing and evolving agents at all scales, from organisms to whole societies, and, increasingly, software and machines."[7]

EMERGENT STRATEGY

Emergent strategy is based on the fundamentals of CAS, but the vocabulary reflects an operating or management focus rather than the behavior of natural systems. By embracing an emergent strategy, public healthcare systems, local education, and environmental initiatives can become more

7. Krakauer, D. C. 2025. *The Complex World: An Introduction to the Foundations of Complexity Science* The Sanata Fe Press, p. 19.

agile and effective in meeting the evolving needs of a targeted population or specific social objective.

Applying an emergent strategy based on CAS creates a system that is based on:

- A customer-centric focus
- Decentralized decision-making
- Local stakeholder inputs and networking
- Real-time performance data
- Focus on positive change (as opposed to problem examination)
- Dynamic operating adjustments
- A culture of continuous learning and adaptability.

These characteristics shape the behavior of every living thing, except for humans who cannot accept the simple network-based idea of collaboration and instead act with selfish, excessive self-interest. Every activity in a proper CAS enhances the increased likelihood of survival. While positive outcomes are not always the result, operating adjustments move the organism closer to a better outcome.

One feature that I find particularly effective in emergent strategy is that tasks and responsibilities are assigned based on experience or resources and there is no expectation that one organization is responsible to execute all facets of the entire strategy. This offshoot of the nested hierarchy was pioneered by the Rockefeller Foundation, which has been studying and advancing strategic philanthropy since 1913. As discussed earlier, much of the early design and development of emergent strategy was done by Professor Henry Mintzberg.[8] My experiences with several foreign social projects show that the best results are shaped by Mintzberg's emergent strategy with active stakeholders individually responsible for complimentary activities and minimal government involvement. Ideally, government limits its role, if any, to funding the project and reviewing required annual project reporting.

---

8. Mintzberg, Henry, and James A. Waters. 1985. "Of strategies, deliberate and emergent." *Strategic Management Journal* 6(3):257–272.

4

The Mismatch: Why Our Institutions Fall Short

As Buckley wrote in "Society—A Complex Adaptive System: Essays in Social Science":

> "Don't simply blame the individuals involved in policy decisions (although they must shoulder the moral and legal responsibilities); blame the sociocultural structure within which they are enmeshed. Search for the role pressures, the premiums and penalties that result from doing or not doing things in certain ways, the goals held out with associated carrots and sticks, and the tensions generated by the often incompatible demands of peers, family, and superordinates, politicians, and national flag."

SYSTEMS THINKING

Buckley is correct to blame the sociocultural structure and the "tensions" with government for the failings in policy, but we must understand first the underlying system(s). Evolution promoted three systems—biological, psychological, and sociocultural. To understand these systems, I introduce a very useful tool—systems thinking—to provide framework to understand any system, including sociocultural and complex.

A system is composed of successive nested levels of subsystems from which come emergent properties. A system is adaptive in order to deal with the energy, matter, and information that pass through a system boundary or are delivered by a feedback loop. A system is chaotic because our reality can only be explained by the behavior of subatomic particles and the particles we now know can only be explained in terms of statistics and probabilities. Systems should not be thought of as structured or mechanical but rather as components holistically linked by networks and feedback loops. It is this self-directed (bottom-up) linkage between information, networks, and feedback loops that is the foundation for every system that can adapt … to changes in an environment. Man has lost sight of this concept that environments change and man must adapt. Man has put sociocultural considerations ahead of the critically important natural environment. Man has also trapped himself within intellectual boundaries referred to as "silos," restricting the flow of information despite the improvement in network availability. Regrettably, such behavior inhibits interdisciplinary, more innovative thinking and conceptual innovation.

Systems thinking was based on the original work in the field of cybernetics by Norbert Weiner at MIT and others. Cybernetics is the study of control systems and information flows and helped to introduce Claude Shannon's monumental accomplishment, Information Theory, into the field of systems. Wiener showed that the "amount of information, entropy, feedback and background noise as essential characteristics of how the human brain functions,"[1] thereby providing the link between natural systems and information theory. This concept was the basis for John Wheeler's famous paper, "Information, Physics, Quantum: The Search for Links," in 1989 that is commonly referred to as the "It from Bit" paper (which was first presented at SFI). The excellent writer Maria Popova (*Marginalian*) describes Wheeler's paper:

> It from bit symbolizes the idea that every item of the physical world has at bottom—at a very deep bottom, in most instances—an immaterial source and explanation; that what we

1. Dirk Klaas Fokke. 2013. "Information: What Do You Mean? On the Formative Element of Our Universe."

> call reality arises in the last analysis from the posing of yes-no questions and the registering of equipment-evoked responses; in short, that all things physical are information-theoretic in origin and this is a participatory universe." (author's italics)

This information-theoretic concept is also the foundation for the usefulness of AI to explain so much of chemistry, biology, and manmade systems and highlights the importance of understanding the principle of "flow of information" in systems thinking. Flow of information explains the continuous exchange of information between different components of a system to foster adaptability.

To understand today's information-based science, economy, and society, and to plan for the future, we need a concept that integrates the power of systems thinking and a social science model called the "Quintuple Helix."[2] Quintuple Helix explains the information-based knowledge economy, society, and the environment.

THE QUINTUPLE HELIX

The Quintuple Helix consists of five interconnected components or subsystems:

1. Education system
2. Markets
3. Natural environment
4. Civil society
5. Government.

The work of social scientists William R. Catton Jr. and Riley Dunlap in the late 1970s first presented the environment, the fifth system, as part of understanding earth as a system, nearly coincident with Jay Forrester's systems thinking work (1971) that predicted existential environmental issues

2. Carayannis, E. G., and D. F. J. Campbell. 2010. Triple Helix, Quadruple Helix and Quintuple Helix and How Do Knowledge, Innovation and the Environment Relate To Each Other?

by 2050. By the early 1980s, social scientists were integrating natural and social science, which expanded the disciplines of social science beyond simply social factors. This expanded context shifted focus from events to the broader examination of structure, patterns, and adaptive behavior in an ecosystem. According to E.G. Carayannis, a thought leader in sociology:

> The natural environment for the process of knowledge production, and the creation of a new innovation is particularly important because it serves for the preservation, survival, and vitalization of humanity, and the possible making of new green technologies; and humankind, after all, should learn more from nature (especially in times of climate change).[3]

This quote highlights the importance of conceptual innovation in the domains of art and science as the basis for technological innovation, entrepreneurship, economic development, and country level progress or lack thereof.

Carayannis again, "A system with five helixes [subsystems] is not linear; it is a web of interrelationships, different systems, niches, and paths that come together to sustain life. This new model extends the traditional linear chain model to the innovation process and broadens it to incorporate all aspects of society, academia, government, industry and natural environment, thus creating a comprehensive National Ecological System of Innovation."[4] The parallels between adaptive behavior and innovation, and more precisely conceptual innovation, should be apparent to the reader. The adaptive behavior of evolution is nature's system of innovation, which functions without any purposeful engineering and design. All innovation begins with conceptual innovation and that is where we increasingly need to focus to address the current problems humanity faces.

In our modern world, three crucial components of the Quintuple Helix—markets, the natural environment, and civil society—are well documented

3. Carayannis, E. G., and D. F. J. Campbell. 2012. Mode 3 knowledge production in quadruple helix innovation systems. 21st-century democracy, innovation, and entrepreneurship for development.
4. Ibid.

to operate as CAS.[5] *However, two other vital components—government and education—remain stuck in linear, top-down hierarchical structures.* This mismatch lies at the heart of our inability to effectively address environmental and social challenges.

First, let me explain the parts of the Quintuple Helix that are CAS. Markets, if controlled by minimal regulation, incorporate self-directed agents, who combine for advantage (firms) to adapt to economic and market change, utilizing the latest communications systems and technology (networks) to capture monetary gains that may not be derived from causal processes (emergence). The environment is the original example of CAS, with 4+ billions years of proof. Civil society is equally obvious and functions as a CAS. Civil society is just little animals (humans) self-directed, adapting to the environment and their modification of the environment, combining efforts (hierarchy) to establish institutions for efficiency purposes, connecting such agents and institutions by networks and consistently producing emergent results through scientific discovery, the arts, and new technology. John Holland summarizes the point well.

> Markets, languages, and biological cells all fit the [CAS] framework, the agents being, respectively, buyers and sellers, speakers, and proteins.[6]

The modern model of government and education share several features that prevent a more adaptive and self-directed approach consistent with CAS. Their approach is not up to the challenges in the modern world of increased complexity and uncertainty. More specifically, the U.S. government and the public education system:

- Were designed during the early years of the Industrial Age and have not been significantly updated for the current information-centric model of the economy and society.
- Are designed to be top-down chains of command, accountability, and regulation.

5. Kresh, J. A. 2006. *Integrative Systems View of Life: Perspectives from General Systems Thinking.*
6. John H. Holland. *Signals and Boundaries.*

- Use linear systems to effectively manage large organizations to achieve consistency and adequate service levels.
- Have unions that may see changes in organization or management as a threat to their well-being.
- Have no incentives to stimulate change.
- Have a client base (the public) with low expectations for government and its activities (education).

The U.S. government and the education systems have served us well for hundreds of years. With the possible exception of Singapore, the U.S. government is the most successful example of government in human history. However, these models of government and education were developed in the mid-1700s at the beginning of the Industrial Age. In fact, most of the changes since then have been to secure or reinforce the power of the federal government, a top-down hierarchical model, through increased federal laws and regulations. This behavior is completely antithetical to the natural order of things and CAS.

THE THREAT TO MANKIND

Mankind faces the most life-threatening period of change since the Ice Age, which lasted 115,000 years and ended about 11,700 years ago. Ice Age initiated experiences and challenges have trained us well but I believe will be inadequate this time. We face unprecedented uncertainty and complexity:

- We must manage the introduction in the economy of novel AI technology that will complete the transformation of the economy to an information-centric model.
- We face an environmental apocalypse forecasted to begin about 2050.
- Society is demanding greater "equity" rather than "equality" of opportunity.

- Globalization of the economy has changed the nature of worldwide economic development, trade, and related alliances.
- Bad actors are increasing in numbers through the use of network and AI technologies, supported by their financial success and support from China and Russia.

To manage this unprecedented convergence of social, economic, technological, and environmental challenges is what I call the "Crisis in Innovation." We must have the courage to cast aside much of our old models and embrace conceptual innovation in the arts and sciences. The arts and social sciences will provide the new philosophical fundamentals to redefine government and the natural and formal sciences will shape anew the technological innovation and tangible solutions to reshape education and successfully address the environmental issues.

I introduce more on AI in the next chapter so the solutions for government might be easier to understand. A major reason we need conceptual innovation in government is the success, advances, and speed of adoption of AI. With the success to date of AI, the investment capital supporting the technology and the thousands of new AI startups worldwide every year, I am not too concerned with the need for technological innovation. The market is quite successful in seeing opportunity. Where we need work is in developing a system that frames the correct opportunities for conceptual innovation. For that, we need to update or modernize the concept of federal government. Harvard Kennedy School professors Danielle Allen and Mark Fagan share similar but more reserved views. They advocate for thoughtful deployment of AI in governance, emphasizing the potential to enhance decision-making, accessibility, and responsiveness while preserving human judgment through a partnership model.[7] The professors propose an Augmented Collective Intelligence (ACI) style approach reminiscent of their neighbors at MIT, but I go further and propose a reorganization of the federal government.

7. https://www.hks.harvard.edu/faculty-research/policycast/ai-can-make-governing-better-instead-worse-yes-you-heard-right

Note: Markets share all the characteristics of CAS, but the same cannot be said for large multinational corporations. These corporations deserve much of the credit for the higher standard of living around the world, even if not achieved equally in all locations. However, these corporations operate much like governments—top-down hierarchy, highly regimented, and self-serving in many ways. Updating the model for the modern corporation is as much overdue as for the federal government, but that will probably be the theme for the next book in the series.

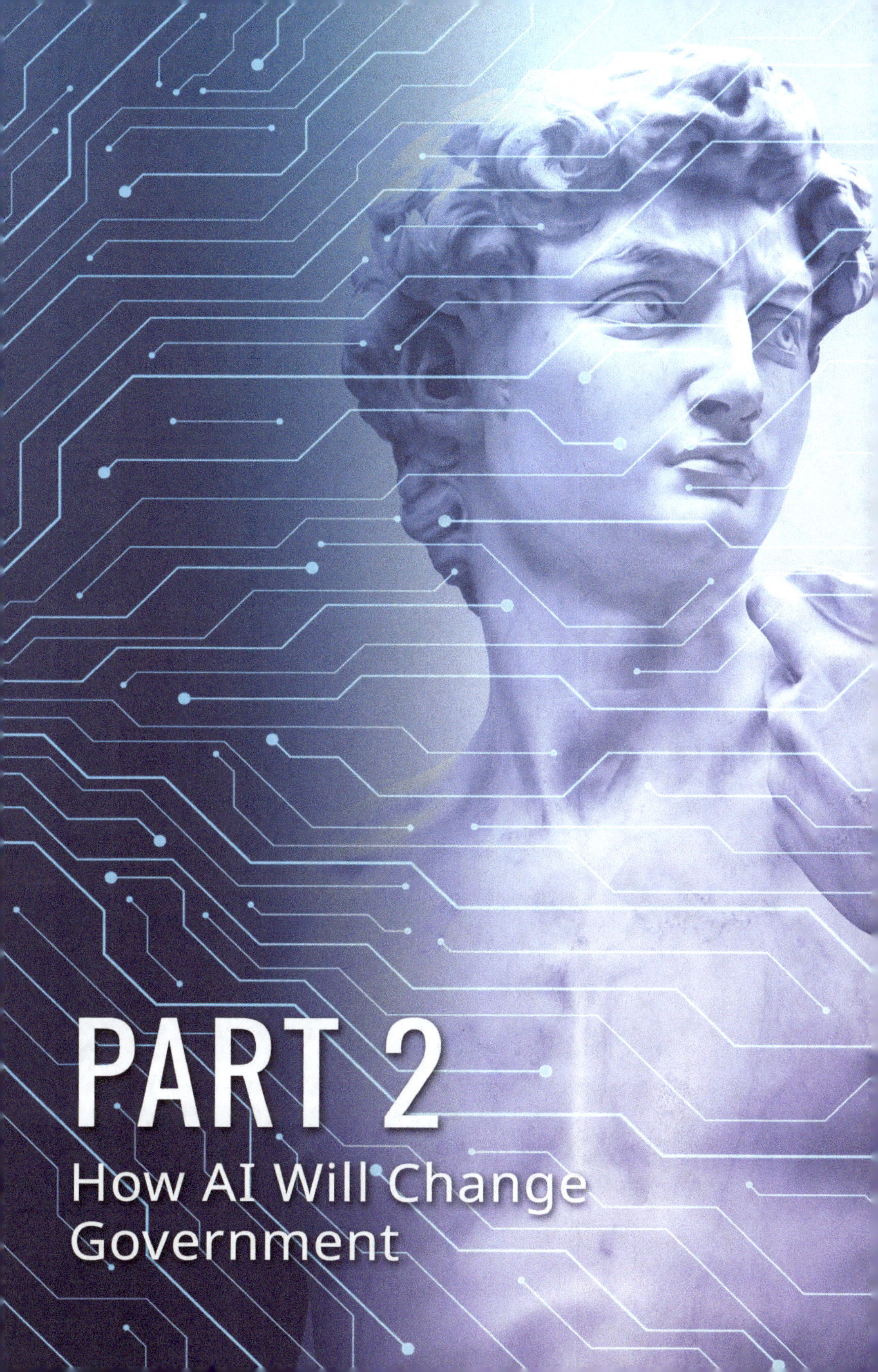

PART 2
How AI Will Change Government

5

The State of Artificial Intelligence

"The hallmark of expertise is no longer how much you know. It's how well you synthesize. Information scarcity rewarded knowledge acquisition. Information abundance requires pattern recognition. It's not enough to collect facts. The future belongs to those who connect dots."[1]

—Adam Grant

INTRODUCTION

There is much research and discussion about industrial revolutions. Industrial revolutions are paradigm shifts in the overall wealth creation model brought about by the convergence of several new significant technologies at the same time. They frequently involve new technologies for energy, materials, or information. These industrial revolutions, beginning in the 1700s, replaced a long-standing agrarian model. The four Industrial Revolutions to date are shown below.

1. https://substack.com/@adamgrant/note/c-98732957?r=qp6q&utm_medium=ios&utm_source=notes-share-action

> 1st—The Industrial Revolution (1760)—substituted manufacturing processes for manual labor
>
> 2nd—The Mass Production Revolution (1870)—fueled by scientific discovery and the widespread adoption of electricity
>
> 3rd—The Information Revolution (1960)—brought on by computerization, networks, and the Internet
>
> 4th—The Knowledge Revolution (2010)—launched by AI and supported by robotics and Internet of Things (IoT).

Beginning with the Third Industrial Revolution, the economy began the transition from a tangible goods model to an info-centric driven economy. AI has accelerated this trend with generative AI creating new "knowledge" in many forms of new content. Buckley in his 1968 book, "Modern Systems Research for the Behavioral Scientist: A Sourcebook," explains this history well.

> Whereas, mechanical systems are determined largely by the physics of energy, more advanced systems are dependent on the flow of information and the environment or context and Shannon's probabilities; so, we are constantly dealing with entropy and what information is stored in a component.

A synopsis of Buckley might be to consider AI as the familiar system of Input—Process—Output.

1. Compute (Input). The computing infrastructure and data management
2. Algorithms (Process). The learning and inference procedures
3. Adaption (Output). The automated outcomes or network of interactions.

Compute brings together the processing power of Nvidia GPU or AMD Ryzen processors and data management infrastructure and tools (cloud computing). The algorithms do the training (learning) and then the manipulation (inference) to produce the outcomes. The adaption defines the purpose of the system to provide answers or inputs for a larger connected system.

The challenge for man is no longer in the physical manipulation (exploitation) of matter, albeit still necessary, but rather now in the exploration of information. This transition may have begun with Gutenberg's printing press and accelerated with computerization, but AI represents the exponential phase of this growth curve and quantum computing will need new vocabulary to describe its contribution. Google's recent announcement about the Willow chip suggests that quantum computing may be available sooner than we think to be paired with AI.

AI—AN UNPRECEDENTED TOOL

Today I believe that AI is a tool comparable to mathematics that will give mankind an unprecedented ability to research and solve problems in science, techno-economic and sociocultural systems, and the environment that heretofore have been unsolvable. Buckley makes clear the missing premise in my argument. We should consider reality to be nested components in which information is stored. The components of reality, whether they be subatomic particles, atoms, molecules, species, cars, technology, or ecosystems, are the storage places for information. If we think about uncovering this reality at scale, twenty-first-century artificial intelligence, paired with vast amounts of data, is the tool we need(ed). Since the time of the English scientist John Dalton (1808) and his introduction of the concept of the atom, science has been documenting this component nature as the information storehouse of nature. If we look at chemistry and biology, and then at medicine and the environment, we now realize why AI has accelerated advances in these sciences and related fields like materials science and drug discovery.

Science is no longer primarily lab-based but now largely the pursuit of knowledge by interdisciplinary information scientists and computer engineers. AI can be simply understood as the combination of pattern recognition and probability. As Pedro Domingos states so well, "Knowledge is often in the form of statistical models, because most knowledge is statistical" (Pedro Domingos, The Master Algorithm). Science and its component nature is the perfect domain for a tool like AI. I cannot resist to use the quote below from Erwin Schrodinger's What is Life? (1944). Every scientist and mathematician should read this short book by the Nobel Laureate (1933). Some say it set the stage for the discovery of DNA by Watson and Crick in 1953.

> The non-physicist finds it hard to believe that really the ordinary laws of physics, which he regards as the prototype of inviolable precision, should be based on the statistical tendency of matter to go over into disorder.

This disorder we call entropy, which is the foundation for Shannon's information theory and the realization that matter at every scale just stores information.

THE STATE OF THE ART (2025)

Fei-Fei Li, the "grandmother of AI" and Stanford professor, makes the point in her book, The Worlds I See, "that the greatest triumphs of AI wouldn't merely be scientific, but humanistic as well." Perhaps without direction or purpose, AI has been moving toward this humanistic objective since the Dartmouth Conference of 1956 launched the modern era in AI. I will forego the earlier contributions of Leibniz, Lady Babbage, and Turing to name a few early pioneers, which is well documented elsewhere and focus on developments since 1990.

In the 1990s and the early part of the next decade, neural networks reemerged as useful algorithms and deep learning became popular when Convolutional Neural Networks (CNN) and Recurrent Neural Networks (RNNs) were introduced. These algorithms allowed for images and audio to be processed, opening the way to a full range of usable multimodal data. Deep learning also emerged as a major tool (algorithm). Over the next two decades, reinforcement learning was combined with deep learning to begin the march toward human-like reasoning by AI, evidenced by AlphaGo's success at chess. Natural Language Processing (NLP) also became popular as the algorithm that moved beyond rules-based approaches to the usage of statistical methods. Google's advances in search engines are a noteworthy example of NLP.

Processors took the limelight beginning from 2000 to 2010 with Nvidia's CUDA processor and Google's TPU offering significantly better performance for AI applications. These advances shaped AI to be as much about Graphic Processing Units (GPU) as new algorithms and datasets. After further advances in computing, in January 2025 at CES Nvidia announced a US$3,000 desktop consumer "supercomputer." This machine is described as 1,000 times more powerful than a standard laptop.

Algorithms also continued to advance with the introduction of Deep Learning algorithms in 2010, which I use to document the beginning of the Fourth Industrial Revolution. Advanced Transformer and Generative AI algorithms followed. ChatGPT was released in November 2022 and successfully demonstrated the consumer market for AI by January 2023 with a reported 100 million users in two months. Advances in the algorithms and consumer apps continue with applications from Claude, Perplexity, and Google to name a few.

The point I make with this short history lesson is that AI is making continuous advances in algorithms, processors, and applications almost every day. AI has now demonstrated that it can be used to explore art, science, engineering, and design at both the commercial or industrial scale and for the consumer.

THE FUTURE AND THE CONSTRAINTS

When I look at the future of technology, the environment, and society, I see it shaped by and reliant on AI. To understand this future, we need to return to the teachings of Princeton Professor John Wheeler who showed us that reality can be understood in terms of information (and energy). Artisanal, hands on lab work will be largely replaced by researchers and engineers using the latest GPUs, datasets, and algorithms to first develop new knowledge, technology, and eventually designs. Then another team will do the sourcing, production, and delivery required. This entire process will be developed, controlled, and monitored by a "digital twin," providing the link for what Jensen Huang, CEO of Nvidia, calls the "two company" model—a digital, info-centric company and a second company that actually produces a physical output, manages a supply chain, or delivers a service. The two company model illustrates one of the two paradigms of AI currently operating—ACI—a term coined at MIT. For the second paradigm of AI, I use the term Advanced Computing, the compute intensive, data-intensive descriptor coined at the NSF. ChatGPT popularized Advanced Computing.

Advanced Computing is like the grandchild of Excel. It completes tasks, generates content, writes and debugs code, and can be creative and artistic in multiple formats. In less flowery language, Advanced Computing is a fantastic tool to improve efficiency, productivity, and decision-making using computational models. Advanced Computing is the source of concern for AI to potentially replace human workers. I would point out someone will be needed to repair the robots and other new AI-based devices and do many other jobs that do not exist today. Then again, maybe the robots will be designed so that a child could do the repair. I am not so concerned by potential job loss. Temporary job loss is a characteristic of the previous three industrial revolutions and an increased number of new jobs did overcome the historic losses. Noted academicians Erik Brynjolfsson and Andrew McAfee document this point in their book, *Race Against the Machine*.

ACI is the networked, collective intelligence of man and AI-powered infrastructure to ideally achieve emergent creativity or at least better results from collaboration between man and machine(s). ACI closely mirrors the idea of a CAS benefiting from a bottom-up hierarchical structure, the ability to adapt, networked connectivity, and the opportunity for emergence. ACI is an advance in the popular IoT networks, which today include 16.6 billion connected devices.[2] This success explains in part the advances in Edge Computing, where the processing is done in the device possibly using SLM (Small Language Models). ACI and Edge Computing also help to explain the development of popular algorithms called Agentic AI or Agentic Models. Agentic Models re-emerged in 2024 to use multimodal data to enable sensing, learning, complex problem-solving, autonomous decision-making, adaptive behavior, and collaboration. Agentic models are also perhaps the most advanced models to demonstrate human-like reasoning without human involvement.

Functional reasoning equal to humans is perhaps a realizable goal, as publicized by Chinese AI leader DeepSeek.[3] In January 2025, they announced a new algorithm that was developed reportedly without Nvidia processors for a few million dollars in a few months. This event caused a record, single-day drop in the market valuation of a publicly traded stock—Nvidia. More importantly, it may have signaled that AI was ready to do what Geoffrey Moore called "crossing the chasm" and switch from an "early adopter" technology for visionaries to an "early majority" technology used by ordinary pragmatists.[4] According to Moore, the valuation bubble popping signals that a possible transition to the early majority stage may commence. Remember also, success is not a given and the "successful" technology could be a derivative of the earlier offerings.

DeepSeek also made clear that the go-to-market strategy will not be shaped exclusively by advanced GPUs and large development budgets in the billions of dollars. AI software may advance in a way similar to traditional

2. https://iot-analytics.com/wp/wp-content/uploads/2024/09/INSIGHTS-RELEASE-Number-of-connected-IoT-devices-vf.pdf

3. https://www.cnbc.com/2025/01/24/how-chinas-new-ai-model-deepseek-is-threatening-us-dominance.html

4. Moore, G. 2014. *Crossing the Chasm.*

SAAS applications such as Salesforce and Dropbox. The focus will be on vertical market applications targeting specific industry needs or tasks such as research, writing, and language translation. These vertical market applications will be developed with smaller budgets and grow rapidly with investment from venture capitalists (VCs). The economics of DeepSeek, the availability to DeepSeek of Nvidia processors, and the use of ChatGPT to accelerate algorithm learning are all unknown and undocumented, but DeepSeek has prompted a reevaluation of the go-to-market strategy in the United States for AI.

One increasingly popular source of data and networked devices is robots. ChatGPT has renewed interest in robots as their new algorithms advance robot functionality. Amazon is a leader in this research. Much as Amazon became the market leader in cloud computing in order to use underutilized compute resources, I think Amazon may become the leader in robots or at least robots for trade and industrial applications. Citigroup forecasts 4 billion AI-robots worldwide by 2050,[5] or about 4 robots for every 10 people. In addition to robots, Jensen Huang sees the adoption of self-driving cars and other applications of "physical AI" accelerated by the recent developments in Agentic AI.

To support the increasing sophistication and scale of AI, the critical path may be the need for data centers and electricity. The need for data centers is shown by developer of ChatGPT, Open AI, and their January 2025 alliance with Softbank, Oracle, and MGX to arrange financial commitments of US$500 billion for new AI infrastructure at Open AI. The project, called Stargate, also includes a technology alliance between Oracle, Nvidia, Microsoft, and Open AI. Such an alliance shows that financial resources will prompt new collaborations to launch large-scale AI projects. And, perhaps we have an explanation for the increased interest in finance to fund sustainable projects particularly in renewable energy.

Energy (electricity), Wheeler's second input to explain reality, is a critical issue in AI development. Data centers supporting AI currently use 3–4%

5. https://www.citifirst.com.hk/home/upload/citi_research/rsch_pdf_30297368.pdf?t

of total U.S. electricity production but could reach as much as 11.7% as early as 2030.[6] I could find no forecast beyond 2030, perhaps suggesting that the results might be a scarily large percentage? *At a minimum, renewable energy has to become an even greater national priority.* Google is reported to be co-developing small nuclear reactors for their data centers. Raghu Madabushi, Director at National Grid Partners, believes that AI models will now be developed to "optimize training and inference processes for energy efficiency, cost effectiveness and sustainability." In fact, a semiconductor processor anywhere in an ACI system should be optimized for energy efficiency and sustainability.[7] As the Spanish say, "ojalá." Let's hope so!

I conclude the chapter with a quote from the *Semafor* newsletter (January 2025).

> This will make the cost of software creation negligible. If you thought software was "eating the world," think again. It was only nibbling at it. We are about to enter an era where everything that can possibly be automated with software will be automated. Next, we'll see a revolution in robotics.

I expect that ACI will be the platform(s) and electricity will be the critical resource.

---

6. https://www.mckinsey.com/featured-insights/sustainable-inclusive-growth/charts/ais-power-binge
7. https://www.fastcompany.com/91254053/25-experts-predict-how-ai-will-change-business-and-life-in-2025

6

Reimagining Government: From Hierarchy to Adaptive Network

> "The history of human civilization reflects a progressive increase in the complexity of large scale behaviors .... When the complexity of collective behaviors increases beyond that of an individual human being then hierarchical controls become ineffective. Hierarchically controlled systems must yield to networked systems."[1]
>
> —Yaneer Bar-Yam

Now we move to applying conceptual innovation to redesign the U.S. federal government model. After developing the new model, I will outline the strategy for the government to pursue. While traditionally one first defines the strategy and then the required organization structure, in this case I believe understanding is improved by reversing the topics.

THE U.S. GOVERNMENT

In Chapter 5, I talked about Industrial Revolutions. Industrial Revolutions are each the perfect example of what I mean by a conceptual innovation.

1. https://necsi.edu/complexity-rising-from-human-beings-to-human-civilization-a-complexity-profile

A transformative discovery in science serves as the basis for new technologies that change the socioeconomic model at scale. Erik Brynjolfsson (Stanford) and Andrew McAfee (MIT) point out significant social unrest immediately precedes or accompanies the start of an Industrial Revolution, very similar to a phase transition that precedes emergence. Perhaps the historic presidency of Barack Obama beginning in 2009, at the start of the 4th Industrial Revolution (4IR), marked such a period in the United States. Perhaps we should consider what Obama foretold. Professor Elvira Martini explains it well:

> The challenge of contemporary society is that of planning possible paths for the future. In the current scenario of hyper connection, men and technologies and human and artificial intelligence are intertwined in such complex ways as to generate multiple possible futures up to the limit of the capacity of imagination. In particular, it is precisely the frontier of digital and technological changes that obliges social actors and socioeconomic institutions to know how to intercept the dynamism of the transformations taking place, supporting the ability to imagine a desirable future, which goes in the intelligent direction of sustainability, of well-being and the ethical responsibility of one's actions.2

But, we must update the model of government to realize the full benefits.

Since the founding of formal government in the United States, at the start of the First Industrial Revolution, the governance system has been based on two sets of principles:

- Federalism
- Democracy.

With the exception of abolishing slavery and giving women the right to vote, I do not think there have been any other fundamental changes in philosophy of government in the United States. Some might argue that the

2. https://www.frontiersin.org/journals/sociology/articles/10.3389/fsoc.2022.1102815/full

ongoing battle for states' rights demonstrates a vitality, but I think that ship has sailed and the federalists have gained supremacy. Excessive Executive Orders by recent presidents might be evidence. Therein lies the problem. We have the system that Bar-Yam described in the quote at the beginning of the chapter. We have a system of government that is increasingly top-down hierarchical.

We have a system of government that has not been fundamentally reviewed and updated for 250 years. I wonder if we could duplicate the intellectual power and agree on fifty-six representatives for a new Continental Congress (1774). Failing that, I make my proposal in this chapter to update the model for government in the United States.

First, let me define democracy and federalism. The Founding Fathers in the United States looked to balance national unity with states' rights.

> **Federalism**
>
> Federalism establishes a constitutional division of authority between national and subnational entities (states, provinces, regions, cities). Both federal and subnational units of government operate independently. The perception by the citizens of this independence reinforces a sense of democracy and local autonomy. Some powers are shared between governmental units, such as taxation, infrastructure, catastrophe management, law enforcement, and public health. Other responsibilities, such as national defense and foreign relations, are intended to be exclusively federal responsibilities.
>
> **Democracy**
>
> Democracy intends for government to be derived from the consent of the governed as determined by free and fair elections for the responsible representative officials. Certain rights are protected, including freedom of speech, freedom of religion, ownership of property, protection by the law.

According to the *Oxford Academic*, "Comparative analysis of successful and challenged federal democracies yields valuable lessons and best practices. Successful systems often demonstrate a strong commitment to constitutionalism, effective intergovernmental relations, robust mechanisms for conflict resolution, and a political culture that values compromise and cooperation."[3] In contrast, in the United States, recent federally elected administrators (presidents) have preferred an increasing use of government by fiat or executive order.

Federal democracies also generally support private enterprise as the engine for economic development, job creation, and improved living standards. Introducing the perspective of CAS helps to explain the high economic growth and success of democratic countries such as Germany, the United States, Canada, Australia, and Switzerland. To reiterate what was introduced in Chapter 3, the CAS framework explains the interactions in a system by explaining the self-directed and adaptive interactions of the agents, elements, and the environment. The interactions provide an exceptional level of system resilience and can generate emergent behaviors that may be unpredictable but beneficial. A "networked" infrastructure accelerates these outcomes. Note that the U.S. economy is a CAS, but the federal government is not.

GOVERNMENT AS A COMPLEX ADAPTIVE SYSTEM

As we consider how to reshape or redefine the U.S. government, we take on a conceptual innovation of enormous consequence. Today the federal government might generously be described as:

- Clear, achievable goals
- Data-driven plans
- Defined roles and accountability
- Rigorous impact evaluations.

3. https://doi.org/10.1093/cesifo/ifm018

Sounds terrific, except that it is an outdated top-down hierarchy designed to control with more concern for form than substance, data collection that will never be used, with rigorous evaluations that focus on government objectives rather than the benefit to the citizenry. And in addition to all these shortcomings, the paramount government objective today looks to be self-interest to ensure the re-election of the standing politicians.

I believe we should draw from the principles of CAS to find the conceptual innovation(s). My objective is to create a new philosophy of government that is the foundation for a new strategy for the United States in the twenty-first century. I want to return the American government to its original democracy—an adaptive, decentralized decision-making organization, with constructive and interconnected agents and a focus on the future benefits for the citizenry. This approach is an example of "emergent strategy" and I develop this theme over the next several chapters.

Why do I believe that CAS and emergent strategy are the model for the vision? All natural systems are CAS. Nature has evolved and survived operating with the five principles of CAS (as described in Chapter 3) for 4+ billion years. A more than sufficient test period that produced successful CAS in markets, cities, and the environment. What better model could I choose to update federal democratic government in the United States? In this chapter, I define the vision for the United States, and in the next chapter, I outline the new strategy and reorganization of federal government.

Two other points need to be made before we get into the explanation for the new government model. The earth is a finite, limited resource that some analysts say we have exhausted or perhaps already overdone. Extreme events, sea level rise, and increased CO_2 levels might be cited as evidence. My point—we need more effective government to urgently address these environmental issues, even if some politicians do not see the merit. This brings me to the second point. As Thomas Jefferson wrote in the Declaration of Independence about inalienable rights, all humans have the rights to "life, liberty and the pursuit of happiness." Perhaps it is the behavior of top-down hierarchies or bureaucracies or unaccountable managers, but today the U.S. government is more focused on regulation enforcement, risk reduction, and winning the next election than it is on serving the citizenry and fostering "life, liberty and the pursuit of happiness." Hopefully, my conceptual innovation in federal government will be responsive to these concerns.

A NEW APPROACH TO GOVERNMENT

Let's begin by looking at the five key features of CAS and where the U.S. federal government has shortcomings. The five features of CAS are: 1) Self-directed, 2) Nested Hierarchies, 3) Adaptive, 4) Networked, 5) Emergence.

1. Self-directed. All behavior by living things is explained by the explore–exploit model, which is the foundation for self-directed behavior. Historically, self-directed behavior focused on survival and reproduction. To enhance survival, all pursuits begin with exploration and an iterative approach to ensure survival. Mistakes were expected and tolerated and activities were designed not to necessarily achieve the objective but to advance toward an objective without loss of life. Once the exploration was deemed successful, then there was a transition to exploitation and the stomach was filled, the thirst quenched, or the family expanded.

   This explore–exploit behavior is now considered best practices in entrepreneurship and corporate new product development. Entrepreneurship uses a minimum viable product (MVP), an operating model with the minimum required functionality, to test market attractiveness, and customer satisfaction. As testing continues, the objective is to get sufficient traction to predict new customers per dollar of customer acquisition cost. As soon as this ratio is determined, the seller transitions from explore to exploit and significantly increases their investment in customer acquisition to exploit the opportunity. MVP is only one of many uses in entrepreneurship of the explore–exploit model, which perhaps explains the widespread success of entrepreneurship.

What does this history or biology lesson teach us about government? Perhaps it is an easier question to answer if I ask why it takes ten years to approve an extension to the electricity grid in the United States or to approve a new drug. Why are we so concerned today with risk? I do not think it is that we know more and are better able to judge risk. I think it is that the government at all levels is in a risk avoidance frame of mind, perhaps because information and "bad news" today is readily available. I also think that the government unduly complicates decisions by including social and business concerns. Not every government decision requires considerations of DEI and job creation. Some do, but not every decision.

What would a better decision-making framework look like? Good strategy, operations, and management always begins first with the vision statement and the values. What should the fundamental values in the United States be? I would list:

- Serve the individual citizen
- Ensure equal opportunity
- Foster democracy
- Provide free markets
- Maintain strong national defense
- Restore the environment.

If a proposed law or regulation does not conflict with the six values, the necessary standard for federal legislation is met. The challenge with such a framework is whether it would allow us to correct the current situation.

As a principle, the government needs to recognize that the situation is so complex and so "real time" that we need to be more adaptive, more comfortable with iterative advances toward a sociocultural objective and more willing to permit self-directed solutions to be tried. This philosophy is fundamental to CAS theory.

On many government decisions, we could do very good evaluations and decision-making based on ML models and digital twins. Digital twins are virtual replicas of objects, systems, and processes that use historic and real-time data and analytics to simulate, monitor, and optimize real-world solutions. These models predict outcomes, test theoretical scenarios, and improve decision-making in all facets of operations from design and production to after-sale service and maintenance. On any proposed government project (not related to national security), the government would be required to build a digital twin model and disclose the project model to let people do their own evaluations of risk, cost, resilience, and reliability. The government could develop their own models to document their justification and then citizens could change assumptions to evaluate the government proposals. Government transparency would sky rocket, project costs would probably go down with public scrutiny, and understanding of government projects would probably increase. Citizens could even monitor the decisions in real time with the same digital twins used to develop the proposals. Effectively, we would have a digital model of the explore–exploit behavior for government. We would probably need a dollar cutoff, whereby only projects with an estimated cost of US$10M or maybe US$100M or more require the public digital twin process. Electricity grid expansion and new drug development would clearly qualify.

2. Nested Hierarchies. The U.S. federal government operates within a structure dictated by the Constitution and federal laws with little autonomy or positive benefit from its hierarchical structure. The organization structure is inflexible and not designed to change to accommodate new needs or events.

   Top-down hierarchies exist in large part as the means to control information centrally to ensure power and authority through an imposed asymmetry of information. Historically government offered an economic benefit through the low-cost centralized storage and distribution of information. As networks continue to proliferate and computing and information capture is further decentralized, for example, to the sensors in an Internet of Things (IoT) network, top-down information hierarchies, such as governments, become less and less necessary. ACI will only accelerate this trend.

The "organization" of CAS is explained by "nested hierarchies." A nested hierarchy refers to the organization of systems within systems, where simpler systems are combined to achieve increased functionality or purpose. The inability to build a nested hierarchy, in part as a result of laws, may explain the apparent absence of economies of scale in government. Economies of scale document the concept that average unit cost declines with volume as fixed costs are distributed over greater production volumes. The U.S. federal budget and the Gross Domestic Product (GDP) from 1975 to 2019 (St. Louis Fed) show that the federal budget as a percentage of GDP has increased from 18.0% to 20.5%. (In fairness to the government, I excluded the years influenced by COVID (2020–2023), although I think the COVID spending was grossly excessive by the Biden Administration after 2020.) Given that the government budget is largely fixed costs, one would have expected the dollar budget as a percentage of GDP to have declined dramatically given that the compounded growth rate for the U.S. GDP was an overall robust 5.95% and the economy grew from US$1.685T to US$21.43T from 1975 to 2019. This logic is called "economies of scale." The implicit assumption here is that the budget spending is designed to foster the overall well-being of the citizenry as measured, for example, by growth in GDP, but the fundamental economic principle of economies of scale should still apply.

To reduce government expenses in a way consistent with CAS and nested hierarchies, I would transform the government into Jensen Huang's two-company model. One government website would be the customer service portal for citizens for every agency or department. Sort of like shopping on Amazon with products, services, problem resolution, and educational and training material. No Prime Video! A common interface across the government would be much appreciated by the citizenry. The other service portal would serve the government employees' needs, with administrative support such as budgeting, project management, grant NOFO preparation and submission review, the digital twin application for new projects, and limited upward reporting. Every agency and department (except maybe Defense) would use the same platform and applications, which would create lower operating costs, lower training costs, and software updates and enhancements shared across the federal government.

Such an approach is available to state, city, and local governments. GovPilot (https://www.govpilot.com/) offers 125+ applications to support the administrative requirements of subnational governments. The most popular applications include code enforcement, construction permits, Freedom of Information Act Requests, and Geographic Information System (GIS) mapping. CivicPlus (https://www.civicplus.com/) offers the citizen-facing software platform for governments, with applications ranging from mass notifications, 311 CRM services, to a single starting point portal for residents, records request, and codification--full citizen customer service in one software solution. Insight Partners, a venture capital company, acquired a majority stake in Civic Plus in 2021 for US$290M. Insight describes CivicPlus as the "first and only Civic Experience Platform." These two market leaders segment the market for subnational government software services as I proposed for the federal government. In the smaller federal government that I propose, perhaps my "two company" software approach could be more easily adopted by the federal government.

ML also is playing an early role in redefining government administration. A story I read recently talked about a city loading all the building code into a ML application. When the architect loaded their plans in the system, visual imaging software would review the drawings against the building code and issue an approval or comments in 1–2 days compared with the months required today. This private company app is being tested. Onebrief (Onebrief.com) is another example of a company developing a vertical market app (platform) for the federal government at the Department of Defense (DOD). Their one-sentence vision statement explains their purpose:

> From the smallest staff work to the largest OPLANs, Onebrief brings faster decision cycles, enables collaboration at scale, and helps every staff section do more with less.

They go on to say:

> Onebrief is a hub for all users to complete all workflows. Build plans and products at record speeds.

The case of Onebrief highlights the very active programs in the DOD to adopt AI/ML. The DOD allocated funding for AI/ML initiatives of US$1.8 billion in its fiscal year 2025 budget for AI-enabled capabilities, including mission-critical applications, such as autonomous systems, real-time decision-making tools, and enhanced cybersecurity measures for modern warfare. Warfare brings a clarity of purpose although not always a clarity for vendor selection or funding.

GovTech spending, public sector technology spending (excluding defense) for public infrastructure, service delivery, ICT, administration, and community engagement globally, totaled US$606B in 2024 and will reach US$1.42T by 2034, an annual growth rate of 8.41%.[4] Recently Germany announced a €500 billion (Euros) stimulus package for infrastructure and defense spending, but with barely a word on AI/ML. Clearly, the more adaptive subnational governments are the thought leaders in this space.

Note: An additional benefit from government-wide applications is that the government could become the first customer for software vendors, thereby supporting private sector new business development and job

4. https://www.startus-insights.com/innovators-guide/govtech-outlook/

creation and even modeling best practices in the use of software and AI for operations and decision-making at scale.

3. Adaptive. The federal government today does not manage itself with adaptability as a primary objective, partly because the primary focus is not on serving the citizenry. Institutional rigidity, processes slowed by rules, procedures and politics, and the need sometimes for formal negotiation all characterize government operations today. Despite the increased uncertainty and complexity of the current period in history and the increasing frequency of extreme natural events like earthquakes, forest fires, and hurricanes, the government has not reorganized to be more adaptive and responsive. The top-down hierarchy managed by politicians and political appointees is the antithesis of self-organizing CAS. Bicameral legislatures and judicial reviews further slow the process and interfere with adaptive behavior.

For the government to operate in a more responsive approach, we need to define the "strategic" objectives for the country. That is the purpose of the next chapter. In the meantime, the government could make more use of prototyping and do more with digital twins to be more adaptive. John Holland explains the point simply.

> Because the agents incorporate adaptive mechanisms, the systems continue to innovate. In other words, the mechanisms of change are primarily mechanisms of exploration rather than exploitation.[5]

To implement such an approach, the federal government needs to:

- Create a culture of experimentation
- Implement a government-wide mandate to adopt design thinking and its human-centric focus
- Prototype at the policy development stage
- Better match the national research labs to the national priorities through the strategy described in the next chapter.

5. John H. Holland. *Signals and Boundaries.*

In February 2011, President Obama released "A STRATEGY FOR AMERICAN INNOVATION" and under an earlier Executive Order,[6] required:

> federal agencies to design cost effective, evidence-based regulations that are compatible with economic growth, job creation, and competitiveness The Order emphasizes the principles of public participation, integration and innovation, flexible approaches, and scientific integrity. It also includes a provision on retrospective review, which asks agencies to submit a preliminary plan within 120 days to determine whether any regulations should be modified, streamlined, expanded, or repealed so as to make the agency's regulatory program more effective or less burdensome.

Notice that the focus of this Executive Order is to "Improve regulation and regulatory review." If we really wanted an adaptive style government focused on the citizen's needs, design thinking would be standard operating practice. Such an approach would instill a focus on the "customer" (citizenry) and not prioritize regulations and would recognize the need for trial and error exploration and prototyping. More on design thinking is available in my first book.[7] The point here is that in this modern world, the government needs to be more human-centric in order to better understand human needs in this increasingly complex world. To support such an approach, we could reduce regulation.

4. Networked. A defining feature in complexity is what *Nature* magazine calls a "multiscale architecture" or hierarchy, ranging from the molecular level to ecosystems and every classification from molecules to species. At each level, we find functional specialization to problem solve to enhance the survival of the living unit whether it be a cell, tissue, or species. *Here we see the collective problem-solving and cooperation characteristic of CAS that is the foundation for the second techno-economic paradigm ACI.* This collective problem-solving uses a natural system

6. https://obamawhitehouse.archives.gov/sites/default/files/uploads/InnovationStrategy.pdf
7. Hacker, R. H. *The Second Renaissance: AI Is Transforming Science, Technology and Entrepreneurship.*

of networks throughout the hierarchy to exchange energy, matter, and information to shape the biochemical matter required by the organism for survival. This reliance on the network points out two shortcomings in government:

- The government is not designed with a network to foster an exchange of relevant information or data between different nodes (agencies) in the network
- There does not appear to be adequate funding for the Cybersecurity and Infrastructure Security Agency (CISA), the organization responsible for the federal government network infrastructure and its future design and development. The 2025 budget was disclosed as approximately US$3B, compared with discretionary spending at the department of Agriculture of US$31.6B. Burying this agency within Homeland Security might be logical from an organizational stand point, but not in terms of the critical function of the CISA to support a robust network operating model.

These weaknesses support instead a siloed and outdated view of the world and unnecessary restriction to available information. When considering the network paradigm applied to manmade systems, Brian Arthur describes it so simply, "every system is multifactorial, dynamic, nonlinear and networked to store and transfer information."

The notable exception is the U.S. government managing the richest, most powerful country on earth.

5. Emergence. Emergent behavior cannot be predicted by examination of a system's individual parts.[8] "Emergent phenomena can manifest in hierarchical structures, with these properties or patterns being qualitatively different from the components that compose them .... It [emergence] underscores a dynamic origin of novelty, development, and even the evolution of complex systems, signifying creativity in-

8. https://www.thwink.org/sustain/glossary/EmergentBehavior.htm

herent in life."[9] For example, we can think of evolution or culture as the accumulation over time of genetic mutations or ideas respectively. Emergence is produced from self-directed, adaptive behavior in nested hierarchies. This simple concept is the basis for the emergent strategy that shapes the required conceptual innovation to redefine federal government.

David Krakauer, the current President of Santa Fe Institute, illustrates emergence through the history of mathematics. Mathematics began with simple geometry but eventual derived calculus and chaos theory, demonstrating properties that are not properties of the parts. Another historic example was the birthing of government by the Sumerians over 6,000 years ago and eventually producing the American federalist democracy. But, federal systems rely on hierarchical structures, regulations, and centralized authority to ensure compliance and accountability. Such an approach restricts the natural tendency for adaptability, self-directed behavior, emergence, and the "evolutionary" advance of the system. The founders of the United States had it right when they stressed state's rights as a requirement, but over time that principle has been steadily eroded. Consequently, federal government in the United States has lost almost totally its adaptability.

For government to take advantage of emergence, we would need to

- delegate more authority to local and other subnational, self-directed units and governments
- adopt self-organizing as a method to address urgent problems
- foster more cross-agency collaboration with real-time data exchange
- support a culture that recognizes uncertainty, risk, and failure.

9. F. Capra and P. L. Luisi. 2014. *The Systems View of Life: A Unifying Vision.* Cambridge: Cambridge University Press. https://doi.org/10.1017/CBO9780511895555

TIME TO MOVE ON

Before I move on to develop a new strategy for the U.S. federal government in the next chapter, I need to make one point in closing this chapter. All animal and natural behavior and successful research, design, and entrepreneurship follows the five principles of CAS. This similarity was explained by child development researcher Jean Piaget, who showed us that learning is a four-step process of passion, discovery, creativity, and invention. Passion harnesses the energy to pursue a problem/purpose. Discovery collects the information and knowledge to shape an understanding. Creativity is the process of recombining the existing components into new solutions. And, invention produces the tangible solution to a problem. *If you stop to think about it, the fundamental process of research, design and entrepreneurship follow the same four-step process.*

Why would the most powerful government in the world, the U.S. federal system, be an outlier and not a CAS. The answer is that this U.S. system has "successfully" met every challenge from wars to hurricanes, financial crises, and social unrest for almost 250 years. In simpler terms, the vast majority of people's lives are better. *I am proposing a new strategy for the U.S. because I do not think the system as currently designed can meet the challenges ahead* and make effective use of AI and ML to ensure a higher standard of living in a livable environmental setting. As we start the Second Renaissance, we should revisit the most fundamental assumptions we have and consider an update to federal government. The question is whether the government and its elected leadership recognize the need and can adjust to a new "model" based on CAS.

Reading my own writing here, perhaps I should have called this book "The Second American Revolution." I am not sure we have the will nor the leaders to redefine government as I see the need. Whether you agree with their proposals, Presidents John Kennedy and perhaps Ronald Reagan were the last two visionary presidents, albeit with very different agendas. In fairness to both, they were separated by about forty years when they served. About 30+ years have passed since Reagan and *we are urgently in need of another visionary president in the United States.*

7

Federal Governance in a Networked World

"To be governed is to be at every operation, at every transaction noted, registered, counted, taxed, stamped, measured, numbered, assessed, licensed, authorized, admonished, prevented, forbidden, reformed, corrected, punished. It is, under pretext of public utility, and in the name of the general interest, to be placed under contribution, drilled, fleeced, exploited, monopolized, extorted from, squeezed, hoaxed, robbed; then, at the slightest resistance, the first word of complaint, to be repressed, fined, vilified, harassed, hunted down, abused, clubbed, disarmed, bound, choked, imprisoned, judged, condemned, shot, deported, sacrificed, sold, betrayed; and to crown all, mocked, ridiculed, derided, outraged, dishonored."[1]

—Proudon

1. O'Hara, K., W. Hall, and V. Cerf. *Four Internets: Data, Geopolitics, and the Governance of Cyberspace.* Kieron O'Hara, Wendy Hall, and Foreword by Vinton Cerf.

INTRODUCTION

Every Industrial Revolution is naturally disruptive to the economy, technological norms, and sociocultural practices. Today we face an unprecedented convergence of such factors in the Fourth Industrial Revolution with the addition of the environment as a threat we cannot ignore. All of this is made more complex by the effects of widespread network connectivity, network effects, and real-time information availability. Not to end this litany of concerns prematurely, we have artificial intelligence poised to replace human reasoning and more money to finance tech startups than ever before. According to *Statista*, U.S. venture capital firms have increased assets under management (AUM) from approximately US$232B in 2009 to an estimated US$1.4T in 2025. Last, but not least, China constantly flexes its muscles around the world with a range of positive and negative activities that the United States has not had to face since Khruschev was Premier of Russia in the 1960s. Vinton Cerf and colleagues summarize the situation well:

> The Internet has a particularly powerful role to play in this, facilitating globalization and expert systems, undermining traditional practices and hierarchies, and disintermediating existing practices.[2]

To face these challenges, the United States has a form of government launched in 1787 and fundamentally not updated since. We need a national recognition to clearly set the national priorities to develop more quickly the resources, infrastructure, and funding to successfully reshape federal government for the Second Renaissance. The fundamentals for such a restructuring come from CAS theory. I close this proposal with a quote from Albert Camus, "Real generosity toward the future lies in giving all to the present."

TWENTY-FIRST CENTURY FEDERALISM

Years ago, I read that "government has policy because they do not have a strategy." A more considerate examination of policy is this definition, "a

2. Ibid.

system of laws, regulatory measures, courses of action, and funding priorities concerning a given topic promulgated by a governmental entity or its representatives."[3] Note, no mention of citizens or social or economic objectives. Such an approach does not take into consideration what Nobel Laureate Friedrich Hayek described as "spontaneous order," "systems where the elements that make up a greater whole do not interact in a linear fashion and where the number of elements and the character of their interaction may be too vast for them to be comprehended by scientific observers."[4]

Federal policymakers are limited to the information they capture, process, and analyze whereas a market or an ecosystem can have millions of agents all motivated to monitor natural and manmade risks, look for opportunity of all types, and explore ways for better lives for themselves and their families. Such systems are the self-directed, adaptive, networked systems we call CAS. To quote John Holland:

> Adaptation by recombination of "building blocks" is a continuing process at all levels, and coevolution clearly has a central role in this continuing adaptation. Any time a new kind of agent appears, there are multiple opportunities for new interactions that modify temporary local equilibria.[5]

If we need to have government, then it should be as close to the citizen agents as possible so as to maximize the natural benefits of the local network—what we call cities or counties in the United States. If we nest these organizations in a hierarchy, we create states or regional development agencies. Such nested hierarchies should only provide services where there are economies of scale or collective benefits (such as multi-county pollution management or law enforcement). *Consequently, we should minimize central planning, federal regulation, and the "services" provided by the federal government.* Instead, we should look to rely more on the government closest to the people with the most current, relevant information. The "real time" government. The significance of this governance model lies in its

3. https://mainweb-v.musc.edu/vawprevention/policy/definition.shtml
4. Pennington, M. Hayek (2020, July 29) on complexity, uncertainty and pandemic response.
5. John H. Holland. *Signals and Boundaries.*

ability to enhance community engagement, inclusivity, and responsiveness to local needs, thus fostering a more equitable and participatory political environment. Historically, bottom-up governance structures have emerged from grassroots movements and sociopolitical ideologies advocating for empowerment and collective action. These movements, ranging from the Civil Rights Movement to the Women's Rights Movement and contemporary environmental initiatives, have achieved the emergent results expected in CAS. These movements are some of the most noteworthy accomplishments of the last 200+ years in U.S. history, all driven largely by citizen initiatives with little or no federal government support or management.

Nobel economist Elinor Ostrom advocated for polycentricity in place of hierarchical government. To paraphrase Ostrom, in polycentric systems, multiple governing bodies at different scales coexist and operate, which can lead to more responsive and efficient governance. These systems tend to have higher absorption capacities because they maintain institutional diversity and can address different issues at varying scales, unlike rigid hierarchical structures that may become inefficient and slow to respond to change. It is this rigidity and slowness to respond and adapt that most concerns me about the current form of federal government.

THE FEDERAL BUDGET

According to the U.S. Treasury, in the last 50 years, the federal government budget has run a surplus four times, most recently in 2001. The accumulation of these deficits represents the U.S. national debt.[6] The most recent data available (Figure 2) shows federal government spending of US$6.75T, revenue of US$4.92T and an annual deficit of US$1.83T. Only China and Japan have annual government budgets that exceed just the U.S. deficit.

The pattern of deficit management in the U.S. government is shown in Figure 3.

6. https://fiscaldata.treasury.gov/americas-finance-guide/national-deficit/

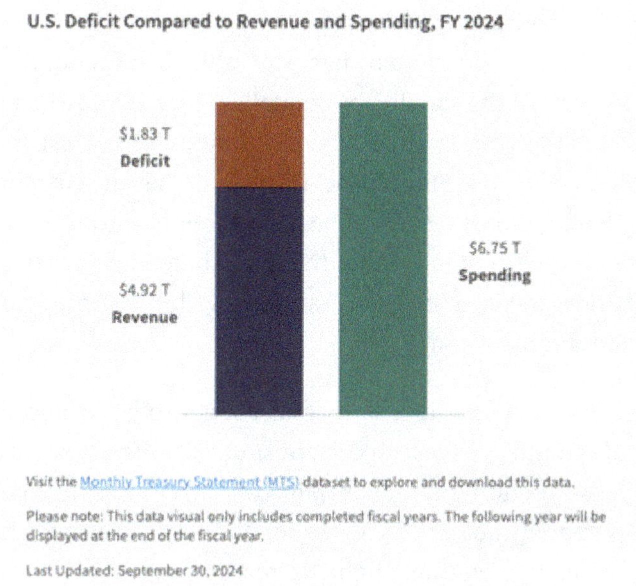

FIGURE 2. **U.S. Deficit compared to revenue and spending, FY 2024.**

Source: https://fiscaldata.treasury.gov/americas-finance-guide/national-deficit/

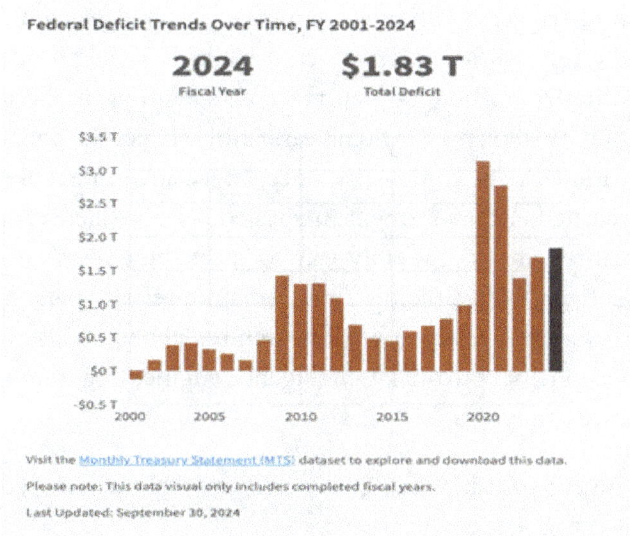

FIGURE 3. **Federal deficit trends over time, FY 2001–2024**

Source: https://fiscaldata.treasury.gov/americas-finance-guide/national-deficit/

For the last 20+ consecutive years, the federal government has spent more than it takes in. The government has been able to successfully borrow in large part because of the stability of the dollar since 1971 (when the United States went off the gold standard), dollar liquidity as international trade paid in dollars expanded, the dollar as the "safe haven" currency and the Fed as the "lender of last resort" to back up foreign central banks with distressed economies.[7] In other words, the world had no choice but to finance the United States to perpetuate the "safe haven" dollar (USD) currency and the world economic system.

I would recommend for the U.S. federal budget to be balanced, for revenue to equal spending, except in certain situations. Those situations might include defense spending under certain conditions. Remember, President Roosevelt prepared the United States for WWII before the war was ever declared and such spending might be required again. The other exception might be a national emergency such as the COVID pandemic (March 2020).

A balanced budget would include annual defense expenditures (but emergencies could trigger additional amounts). The budget would equal the anticipated revenues less a 0.25% reserve available at the president's discretion. The other rule would be that research spending should equal 1% of the budget (at least for the next ten years until most of the benefit from AI/ML is determined). The complexity, uncertainty, and impact of AI is grossly underappreciated and investment in applied ML for science, engineering, and medical research is the only way to meet the citizen's needs, realize the benefits from the technology, and remain internationally competitive. (More on research in Chapter 6.) Research budget could also be allocated for the development of artificial intelligence engineering to modernize the infrastructure to support AI/ML.

U.S. government spending in 2025 by category is shown in Figure 4.

7. https://www.brookings.edu/articles/the-dollars-international-role-an-exorbitant-privilege-2/

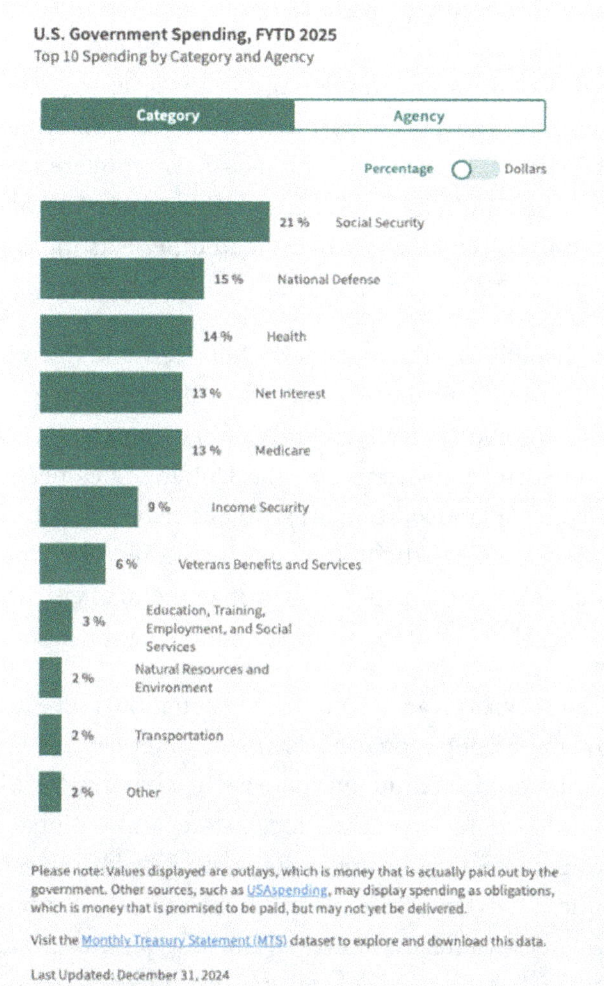

FIGURE 4. U.S. GOVERNMENT SPENDING, FYTD 2025

Source: https://fiscaldata.treasury.gov/americas-finance-guide/national-deficit/

Much of this spending would be transferred to the states or perhaps counties or cities. *Only the departments and functions that remain at the federal level would be funded from the federal budget.* Much of the funding, for example in education and healthcare, would be subnational. The source of funding might be increased local property, sales, or income taxes.

One-time payments would provide a separation allowance to terminated federal employees, perhaps totaling one year's salary and benefits for senior managers and two years for middle- and lower-level workers. There is a cost to reorganization and I believe that we must recognize the years of service of displaced workers and they should be given a preference in new jobs at the federal, state, and city level. Citizen obligations for social security, Medicare, Medicaid, veterans payments, and other existing commitments would be honored as currently obligated.

An additional benefit to reducing federal "services" and the related budget is that it could perhaps stimulate a rollback in the increasing use of Executive Orders and the expansion of federal powers. This trend is categorically wrong!! In the current environment, the United States needs to learn a more self-directed, adaptive, resilient style of behavior, which can only be achieved if government is the bottom-up nested hierarchy of CAS. Such a process would also perhaps better prioritize the management of the increasing number of extreme events by subnational government units.

With increased services transferred to the subnational level, the question becomes how these subnational government units pay for the increased service levels. I would institute an increase in tax rates for high-earning individuals and corporations at the local, state, and national levels, with state and certain federal tax revenues down-streamed based on population headcount. These two tax initiatives would be the first step to be followed perhaps by higher local taxes. However, the first question we might ask is what services do these local people want? Next question, what services do people need? And last, what services are citizens and corporations willing to pay for in higher sales, income and property taxes, and one-time assessments. I think the biggest challenge might be to get the citizenry to pay for environmental safeguards and related quality standards improvement. I would like to think that payment for public education and emergency healthcare and public health would be as obvious as law enforcement, drinking water quality, and parks and public recreation. I live in Miami Dade County. I find that the county government is generally correctly aligned on services for the public, although I would recommend more taxes to fund education and the environment. I also may be jaded by my discretionary income, but I would willingly pay higher local taxes to cover better levels of required services for the county population as a whole.

THE FEDERAL ORGANIZATION

My organization, or more accurately, my proposed reorganization of the federal government is designed not to require any constitutional amendments. As part of the proposal, I think we should legislate an annual balanced federal budget and perhaps a required budget surplus of X% of annual federal revenues to retire federal debt. According to the U.S. Treasury, the federal debt totaled US$35.46T or 123% of U.S. GDP in 2024 compared with US$7.3T in 1990 or 60.8% of GDP.[8] To me, this looks like reckless government spending and I am challenged to understand it. The combined Afghanistan and Iraq wars cost an estimated US$4–7T in the same time period. This leaves another ~US$21T still to explain for the debt increase. How much in federal student loans for college was the net increase from 2004 to 2024? Only US$1.49T. Only US$18.5T left to explain. According to the General Accounting Office, COVID-19 pandemic spending cost US$4.6T, leaving a balance to explain of ~US$14T. We could go on with this analysis, but with US$14T not obviously explainable and US$4–7T devoted to very questionable wars, the need to reduce federal government responsibility, and spending is an obvious and immediate need.

Niall Ferguson, noted historian and Senior Fellow at both the Hoover Institute and Harvard University, proposed the Ferguson Rule. This rule predicts the decline in a country's power and fiscal health when fixed payments of interest and principal on national debt exceed defense expenditures. According to Ferguson, for the first time in almost one hundred years, federal expenditures for debt service totaled US$1.124T in 2024 and exceeded defense spending of US$1.107T. Debt service as a percentage of U.S. GDP has increased from 1.8% in 1989 to 3.1% in 2024. Ferguson recommended

8. https://fiscaldata.treasury.gov/americas-finance-guide/national-debt/

reducing federal deficits without reducing defense spending.[9] I would look to cut out 5% of the defense budget in a one-time hit to eliminate the waste at DOD, which is routinely present in every government agency (or any organization). Ray Dalio, the Founder of hedge fund Bridgewater Associates, has a book for release September 2025, "How Countries Go Broke." To manage a comparatively large U.S. government debt, one anticipates that he will propose for a U.S. debt restructuring along with fiscal management to increase government revenues and reduce expenditures. While Dalio analyzed a reported thirty-five government bankruptcies to reach his conclusions, the more important point is that one of the most sophisticated and successful investors in history felt the need to declare the federal government debt levels a serious and urgent problem. I would add to these proposals for better fiscal management, the need to modernize how we manage the federal government. As described below, I think we need to eliminate certain government agencies and combine others. Combining agencies might break down the silos, improve information exchange, and even foster the kind of collaboration one sees in CAS. In addition to balancing the annual federal budget, I also think that we need to raise taxes in the United States for the top 2% of tax payers and the goal is to raise US$500B per year for ten years. Such an increase in taxes collected would be to explicitly pay down national debt.

Another principle in my approach to reorganizing the federal government is to develop shared federal services. The most obvious areas for shared services are Research and Information and Computer Technology (ICT), which are explained in the next chapter.

I also think that collaboration between government, corporates, and academia needs to be reorganized and expanded. I describe this ecosystem concept in Chapter 15.

9. https://niallferguson.substack.com/p/debt-has-always-been-the-ruin-of

8

The Strategic Reorganization of a Modern Federal Government

> "History affords us many instances of the ruin of states, by the prosecution of measures ill-suited to the temper and genius of their people."
>
> —Ben Franklin, ca.1774

Since the first term of Bill Clinton, I think the United States has been ignoring Ben's warning. I propose a reorganization in the federal government in an effort to better serve the people of the United States.

THE NEW FEDERAL STRUCTURE

The units that remain federal branches and departments are:

- Executive branch
- Legislative branch
- Judiciary branch
- Department of the Treasury

- Department of Defense (consolidated to include the military, security services, and national law enforcement)
- Department of Energy
- Department of the Environment (consolidated to include sustainability, climate tech, national lands and parks, agriculture, food, and water)
- National department for ICT (Information and Computer Technology)
- National Research Institute (modeled on the National Science Foundation to develop new transformative science, engineering and medical science and oversee the Food and Drug Administration [FDA] approval processes).

I would also note that we need a separate department within the new National Research Institute specifically to research and develop new AI/ML. The new ICT department would review, approve, and purchase new algorithms, apps, hardware, and services (cloud, satellite, etc.) for AI and applied ML. Such approved products would then be available for purchase by federal government agencies.

Research and ICT are described in this chapter. Education, Healthcare, Energy, Environment, and Defense are each described in their own chapters. The Executive, Judiciary, and Legislative branches are fundamental to democracy in the United States, so I will refrain from reorganizing or reducing their scale. However, as a matter of good discipline, I would look to put in term limits of ten years for all legislators and judges and limit their retirement benefits based on a matching contribution of an annual percentage of their salaries to a 401K retirement plan. The Department of Justice I would like to put under the Department of Defense (DOD) with all the national law enforcement units, but that might be too controversial. If necessary, it could be a small standalone department like Treasury. I intentionally did not go to the next level of detail and there may be further opportunities for consolidation or assumption of responsibility by subnational governments.

The new ICT Department would have a government-wide mandate, excluding the Department of Defense (DOD), to modernize computer services, AI, and data management. Building on Jensen Huang's two company model, ICT would build apps and infrastructure to serve the citizenry—share, collect and process information, handle federal reporting (e.g., grant reporting), and payments to all of the federal government branches, departments, and agencies. The entire citizen/government interaction would be digital, online, and in real time. The second ICT "company" would handle all the internal government reporting, analysis, follow up, and corrective action. All of this would be digital, online, and in real time, except for the intervention of law-enforcement agencies when requested by the system. This approach is supported by a report from the World Economic Forum on the "govtech" market, the "whole-of-government" efforts to digitalize service.[1]

The logic of this "two company" approach is validated at the subnational level of government where some companies provide software suites for citizen-facing services and other companies provide software to support the internal administrative services of government. CivicPlus, https://www.civicplus.com/, is a leader in serving citizens' needs for subnational governments. CivicPlus' services range from mass notification to 311 CRM and process automation. Venture Capital firm Insight Partners invested US$290M in 2021 in the company to support accelerated growth. OpenGov, https://opengov.com/, is another subnational government software provider offering administrative applications. In 2024, Cox Enterprises, a private equity firm, acquired control of OpenGov for US$1.8B. The scale of the software offerings, the customer bases of these services providers and the amount of outside investment I think validate that the federal government should think about the approach to software I propose. The federal government could install the software vertically by agency and then move to the next agency. Some new software might be needed to allow information exchange between agencies.

The other responsibility of ICT would be to acquire, manage, and maintain the public shared resources that should be available to permit any U.S. citizen or green card holder access to the most modern AI/ML infrastruc-

1. https://govinsider.asia/intl-en/article/govtech-will-be-usdollar14-trillion-opportunity-by-2034-says-wef

ture and datasets. These shared resources would level the playing field by offering free access to databases and ML software so that anyone could develop a product or service for free. Any person or business with taxable revenue of less than US$1M per year and any nonprofit organization would be eligible. Any resultant operating company or product would bear their own costs going forward after development, although maybe an SBA-like program could provide additional federal funding.

The national research organization, which I would continue to call the National Science Foundation (NSF), would share research responsibility with the federal departments of Energy, Environment, and Defense. The NSF would carry out basic research directly and through grant funding in physics, chemistry, engineering, medicine, and education, including the historical initiatives at National Institute of Health. Applied research to move research from proof-of-concept to prototype would be the responsibility principally of the remaining federal agencies—Energy, Environment, and Defense—who could also provide grant funding to universities and corporates for prototype development.

As stated in the previous chapter, Energy, Environment, and Defense would be required to devote at least 1% of their annual budget to research, each agency making their decision on what percentage to allocate to internal development and what percentage to allocate to third-party grant funding for universities and private sector firms. *To focus on and encourage transformative research and avoid iterative, wasteful research, any annual research budget not spent could be rolled over for up to five years.*

An important question that needs to be addressed is the low percentage of any federally funded research that is commercialized through licensing, sponsored research by the private sector, or startups. This comment is equally valid for both federal agencies (and their research labs) and university grant recipients. One way to change the performance would be to change the metrics for college professor evaluation. Most university researchers are not evaluated on their technology being licensed or commercialized by any means. Making such tangible accomplishments a key metric in tenure determination would quickly motivate faculty researchers. To support this goal, faculty, post-docs, and PhD students need more training in entrepreneurship, which is an area that NSF has highlighted before. I would extend the "first commercialization" grant-training program, NSF I-Corps, to be followed by a formal incubator program with US$150,000 in funding per company/project (with no admin offsets by their university) to advance research to prototypes (Stage 2) after successfully completing I-Corps. I would use a committee of venture capitalists from top VC firms to select the projects that participate in this accelerator. VCs would have the right to invest in the projects and have the companies skip this prototype program. Graduation from the accelerator would be a pitch day to VCs with the expectation that some teams would secure additional funding to pursue what the NSF calls the third stage, "technological development," and the private sector calls go-to-market. Perhaps we could ask Y Combinator to organize the pitch day or even run the accelerator at no charge, given their many years of such experience and their excellent results.

Both the I-Corps and the new accelerator program would target the current NSF Key Technology areas:[2] 1) Advanced Manufacturing; 2) Advanced Materials; 3) Artificial Intelligence; 4) Biotechnology; 5) Communications and Wireless; 6) Cyberinfrastructure and Advanced Computing; 7) Cybersecurity; Disaster Risk and Resilience; 8) Energy Technology; 9) Quantum Information Science; 10) Semiconductors and Microelectronics.

The biggest question on national research in my mind is how to pursue medical research and the need for improved healthcare at a lower cost. The United States has the most expensive per capita healthcare costs in an advanced country by a factor of ~2×.[3] Life expectancy in the United States is a significant 4.1 years shorter than comparable advanced countries.[4] Clearly, something is broken!! I think that Health and Human Services should be reorga-

2. https://www.nsf.gov/focus-areas/technology
3. https://www.healthsystemtracker.org/chart-collection/health-spending-u-s-compare-countries/#GDP%20per%20capita%20and%20health%20consumption%20spending%20per%20capita,%20 2022%20(U.S.%20dollars,%20PPP%20adjusted)
4. https://www.healthsystemtracker.org/chart-collection/u-s-life-expectancy-compare-countries/#:~:text=Life%20expectancy%20at%20birth%20in,the%20U.S.%20and%20comparable%20 countries

nized with medical research and drug approval a responsibility of the new NSF and all other human services and their 2024 budget of US$3.24 T (the largest annual federal government outlay) targeted for administrative and operating cost reductions without a reduction in Medicare and Medicaid benefits. All eligible pharmaceuticals should be generics where available!! The target here is not to reduce the number of people legally covered or the quality of their care, but rather to focus on achieving the natural economies of scale that should be derived for an operation of this size.

It is clear that biology and the related medical sciences and engineering will be the most well-funded area of civilian research in the twenty-first century. AI/ML is the perfect tool to manipulate atoms, molecules, genetic material, and the cells that are foundational components of this science. This observation is confirmed by the venture capital community. In 2024, global venture capital investment in healthcare (healthtech, biopharma, and biotech) reached US$67.2B. Such investment shows the growing confidence in AI's ability to revolutionize healthcare solutions.[5] The key will be how to rapidly advance the research to develop and approve therapies. Digital twins are being used to simulate a patient's disease progression. They allow researchers to predict outcomes for patients under different treatment scenarios using fewer participants in clinical trials. This innovation can reduce trial size, cost, and development time. Stanford College of Medicine Dean Lloyd Minor summarizes the future of AI in medicine well, "In addition to its promise for accelerating scientific discovery, AI tools also have tremendous potential for increasing our precision in predicting disease and our efficiency in diagnosing it."[6] Applied ML offers new means to more efficiently diagnose illness at lower cost with fewer tests. A large beneficiary of this potential cost savings would be the national healthcare programs of the United States.

I would propose that the existing Social Security system, Medicare, and Medicaid be maintained at the federal level, with the inflation adjustment scheme to remain in place to honor existing obligations. Perhaps these

5. https://natlawreview.com/article/state-funding-market-ai-companies-2024-2025-outlook
6. https://www.linkedin.com/pulse/synthetic-patients-other-ways-ai-could-revolutionize-lloyd-minor/

services could be rolled into the Treasury department or another remaining federal department to reduce the overhead costs. There are many opportunities to reduce costs in these departments, and as the largest source of government expenditure, further administrative rationalization and automation of these services should be a very high priority. (It is not my intention that by my omission I have overlooked an existing federal obligation, such as veterans' benefits. All obligations for healthcare, disability, and any other form of "basic" human welfare should be honored for the life of current recipients.) Any child reaching the age of twenty-one, would automatically be enrolled in their state contributory plan for retirement benefits and medical coverage upon reaching 70 years of age. The indigent would receive free medical services locally as I hope they are today.

THE REORGANIZATION

The federal government was conceived in the eighteenth century and greatly expanded by President Franklin Roosevelt, before the commercialization of computers and computer networks. The U.S. GDP grew from US$173.52B in 1945 to US$29.T Q4 2024 (FRED), in part demonstrating increased economic, technological, and sociocultural vitality across the country at the individual state and city levels. This success suggests to me that much support is no longer needed from the federal government and can be handled by the states or ignored if the local voters wish. Other outdated federal departments may still serve a purpose but could be scaled down and combined with other departments. Shown below is my proposal to redefine the federal government at the Cabinet level. Currently there are fifteen such agencies.

- Department of Agriculture—combined into the Department of the Environment
- Department of Commerce—closed
- Department of Defense—remains standalone
- Department of Education—closed
- Department of Energy—remains standalone

- Department of Health and Human Services—closed
- Department of Homeland Security—combined into the Department of Defense
- Department of Housing and Urban Development—closed
- Department of the Interior—combined into the Department of the Environment
- Department of Justice—remains standalone
- Department of Labor—closed
- Department of State—remains standalone
- Department of the Treasury—remains standalone
- Department of Transportation—closed
- Department of Veterans Affairs—combined in the Department of Defense.

The Department of Agriculture (FY 25 Budget US$29.2B) should be folded into the Department of the Environment. Natural resource conservation and food safety and regulation are the key functions to be preserved.

Department of Commerce (FY 25 Budget US$11.4B) should be closed and economic and census data collection and patent and trademark registration should be moved to the Treasury Department. Weather forecasting should be moved to the Department of the Environment.

Department of Defense is maintained and described in its own chapter.

Department of Education (FY 25 Budget US$82.4B) is closed with responsibilities assumed by subnational governments. Any desired scholarship programs could be assumed by the Treasury Department. A research budget for Special Education, underprivileged students, and other groups of interest could be managed by the NSF, who historically has sponsored such research in education.

Department of Energy is maintained and described in its own chapter.

Department of the Environment is created and described in its own chapter.

Department of Health and Human Services (FY 25 Budget US$133.8B) is closed with responsibilities assumed by subnational governments. Medicare and Medicaid could be folded into the Department of Treasury until the current participants no longer require payments. Subnational 401K-type programs would cover new entrants and contributions would be obligatory and completely managed by the private sector. Child welfare and family support programs would be delegated to subnational governments.

Department of Homeland Security (FY 25 Budget US$62.2B) would be rolled into the Department of Defense, providing for shared overheads and better coordination and sharing of information. Emergency response to natural disasters and terrorism would be specially targeted for improved response.

Department of Housing and Urban Development (FY 25 US$72.6B) would be closed and responsibilities assumed at the subnational level.

Department of the Interior (FY 25 US$17.8B) would be rolled into the Department of the Environment.

Department of Justice (FY 25 US$37.8B) could be rolled into the Department of Homeland Security and become part of DOD. If this recommendation was deemed too politically sensitive, I would leave Justice as a standalone department.

Department of Labor (FY 25 US$13.9) is closed and responsibilities assumed at the subnational level.

Department of State (FY 25 US$64.4B) remains standalone as currently configured but with greater scrutiny of USAID and similar spending.

Department of the Treasury remains standalone and absorbs the functions described here.

Department of Transportation (FY 25 US$25.4B) is closed. Federal highway development and maintenance and air traffic control would be rolled into DOD as national security priorities.

Department of Veterans Affairs (FY 25 US$129.3B) would be rolled into the Department of Defense.

The Vanguard Megatrends Model[7] demonstrates that technology has been the most significant driver of U.S. GDP growth historically. "The U.S. economy's coming decade will be shaped by a tug-of-war between artificial intelligence (AI) and demographics-driven deficits." For the technology to succeed and offset the negative effects from the aging population, AI must be used for augmentation to increase labor productivity, for efficiency principally through increased automation and lastly through what Schumpeter called "creative destruction" and the resultant transformative innovation. The federal government should have as a principal objective in the reorganization described above to incorporate AI/ML for these three objectives and their economic and operating benefits.

In order to execute this strategy properly, I think we need to reduce federal government to focus on a smaller set of key departments—Energy, Environment, Research, ICT, and DOD. At the same time, I recommend that we return to the historical principle of states' rights and shift more responsibility for health, human services, and education to the states. Such an approach mirrors the nested hierarchy approach of CAS and allows for the local preferences of the citizenry to be better matched to the provided services. Some issues require further thought, such as the national highway system, ports, and some other infrastructure of high national importance. They could continue to be funded by a federal tax on gasoline or electricity, but their administration requires national attention despite few obvious economies of scale. Maybe place this national infrastructure within the Department of Defense?

The next part of the book, Part 3, deals with the key issues and federal departments. It is intended to further explain the strategy I propose. Although Education and Health and Human Services are targeted to be shut down as federal departments, I believe separate chapters are warranted to explain the critically important future of education and healthcare. After that I describe in separate chapters the Energy, Environment and DOD departments of the federal government.

7. https://explore.vanguard.com/megatrends.html

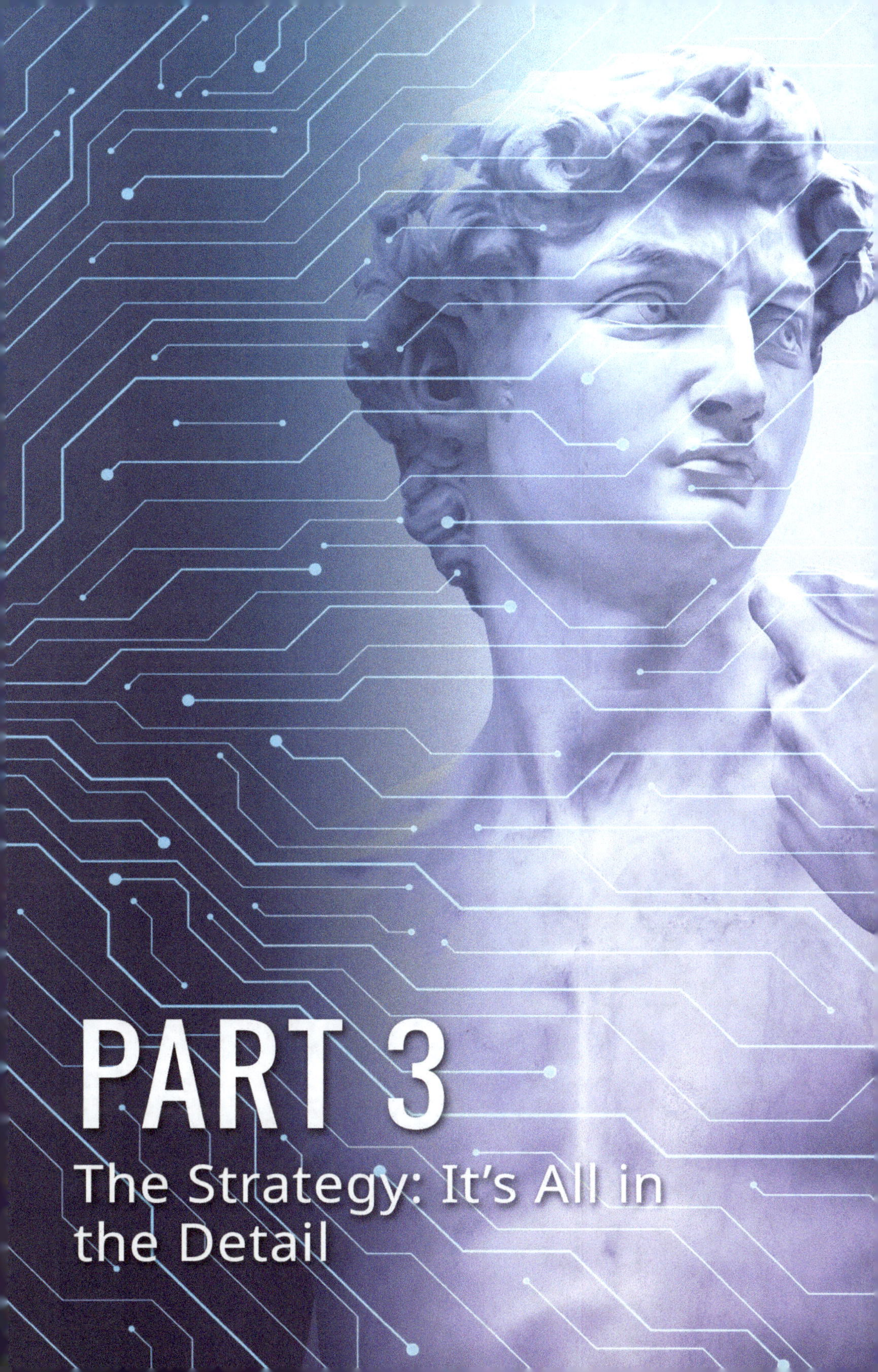

PART 3

The Strategy: It's All in the Detail

9

The Education Revolution: Preparing Minds for Artificial Intelligence and Complexity

> "The hallmark of expertise is no longer how much you know. It's how well you synthesize. Information scarcity rewarded knowledge acquisition. Information abundance requires pattern recognition. It's not enough to collect facts. The future belongs to those who connect dots."[1]
>
> —Adam Grant on Substack

In a recent post on "destroying" America, an author proposed a strategy to simply weaken education, reduce healthcare, and foster racism. In this chapter, I discuss education and in the following chapter, I discuss healthcare. For both services I propose to transfer the responsibility to subnational governments.

To begin this chapter on the modernization of education, we must first return to the physics of John Wheeler. Wheeler showed us that information is reality stored in objects ("It from Bit"). For example, everything about

1. https://substack.com/@adamgrant/note/c-98732957?r=qp6q&utm_medium=ios&utm_source=notes-share-action

the apple is stored in the genetic code of the apple. Beginning with the First Industrial Revolution in the late 1700s, mechanization became another store of information. These new mechanical processes replaced our cognitive processes. The computer only accelerated this process and AI/ML is the most advanced system to date to create and capture knowledge. With these advances in technology, we must rethink where the human cognitive processes can still create value. That is the challenge we face in modernizing education and learning in the twenty-first century.

THE HISTORY OF EDUCATION IN THE UNITED STATES

"Horace Mann, widely regarded as one of the fathers of American public education, was a keen student of the Prussian model. He visited Prussia in 1843 and came back determined to emulate that country's public schools. In Mann's eyes, the purpose of public education was not mainly to raise standards (after all, by 1840 literacy in the northern states had already reached 97 per cent), but to turn unruly children into disciplined citizens. He could not have been clearer that this was for the good of the country, not the needs of the individuals."[2] The system used rote memorization to teach reading, writing, and arithmetic and in the case of the United States to transfer a democratic value system to recently arrived immigrants.

Today, "In the United States alone, there are nearly 14,000 school districts and nearly 100,000 public schools operating in a highly decentralized system. A range of people make decisions that impact a student's experience in school: federal and state policy leaders, superintendents, principals, teachers, parents, and more."[3] Noticeably absent typically are the students themselves, who in my experience frequently are the most open-minded, results-oriented group of possible participants in such a discussion.

2. Matt Ridley. *The Evolution of Everything.*
3. https://acceleratelearning.stanford.edu/story/stanford-initiative-helps-scale-what-works-in-education/

The State of Florida, where I live, has a representative state department of education. Article IX, section 1 of the Florida Constitution establishes the State of Florida's commitment to funding kindergarten through grade 12 education, as follows:

> The education of children is a fundamental value of the people of the State of Florida. It is, therefore, a paramount duty of the state to make adequate provision for the education of all children residing within its borders. Adequate provision shall be made by law for a uniform, efficient, safe, secure and high quality system of free public schools that allows students to obtain a high quality education ....

Related funding is on a per-student basis and includes scholarship support for Charter Schools[4] and home schooling under certain conditions.

Education across the state of Florida and the nation is in a state of flux. I believe it is another symptom of the Fourth Industrial Revolution and the uncertainty that accompanies changes of this magnitude. One group advocates for "career readiness" and the "Future of Work" as the basis for a new approach to education. Another group advocates for the status quo and basically adheres to Horace Mann's nineteenth century philosophy. A third group advocates for a social agenda to shape education. I propose an approach that was introduced to me at the MIT Media Lab and was the basis for the world-renowned edtech project I worked on there—One Laptop per Child (OLPC). OLPC advocated for a connected laptop for each child, freely given to the child and connected to the Internet. *This approach allowed the child to pursue self-directed learning, problem-solving, and collaboration with fellow students.* Teachers could introduce lesson plans or new topics and provide limited web-based resources if they wished. This approach was based on the writings of the child development scholar Jean Piaget and consistent with the thinking of the polymath Herbert Simon.

4. A charter school is a public school that operates independently from a school district. Charter schools commit to obtaining specific educational objectives in return for a charter to operate a school. Charter schools are exempt from significant state or local regulations related to operation and management but otherwise adhere to regulations of public schools—http://charterschoolcenter.ed.gov/what-charter-school

Simon prosed science-based learning balanced with active learning and actionable knowledge for problem-solving. Effectively Simon transposed his seminal thinking on design to education or more precisely learning. Great thinkers frequently produce multidisciplinary applications for their thinking.

LIFE-LONG LEARNING

Piaget, Simon, and many others also set the stage for life-long learning and personalized learning. In all of my formal education from about 1956–1980, I was never formally introduced to either of these topics. The rate at which new information grows prompts me to constantly advocate for my students to be life-long learners. Personalized learning is very individualistic, but Chamath Palihapitiya's system[5] is very similar to my way of learning. His system has five steps:

1. Consume lots of content
2. Develop a point of view
3. Do 1–2 month deep dives
4. Review learnings with smart people
5. Refine your point of view.

I review my learnings (Step 4 above) with my undergraduate students in class. I use a learning method that involves four steps:

1. Read (at least four hours per day)
2. Teach (2×/week)
3. Write
4. Learn.

Writings such as this book tend to demonstrate a certain self-realization, hopefully a "completed" understanding on a topic or theme. Hopefully, it is a refined, valuable point of view. I have been using writing to demonstrate

5. https://chamath.substack.com/p/learn-with-me?r=qp6q&utm_medium=ios&triedRedirect=true

advances in my thinking since my first blog, *Sophisticated Finance*[6] (2006) and on *Medium* since 2014.[7]

MODERN EDUCATION

A concept that I like for a modern school is the Alpha School model.[8] Self-directed learning, active learning, and life skills are the three principles that shape each Alpha School. Personalized learning shapes the student's educational journey. Only two hours a day are spent in the traditional classroom working on core subjects (math, science, reading ...) and 4–6 hours per day are spent on project-based, collaborative learning exercises. Every exercise includes life skills from "public speaking to coding, entrepreneurship, and outdoor education" and character.[9] I would insert individual robotic mentors in the Alpha School model to allow it to scale to public school requirements and further support self-directed personalized learning. Teachers would ideally focus on students with the greatest needs.

An important part of any curriculum in addition to math, science, and philosophy (to teach reading) would be multi-year programs (classroom and sessions) in STEM (Science, Technology, Engineering, and Mathematics) and AI/ML. Beginning with the fundamentals of statistics and coding, the program would include data analytics, predictive, and prescriptive ML, and ACI and/or agentic models. Ideally, there would be opportunities for hands on learning about robotics, edge computing, and multimodal data to enrich the STEM education.

This approach is heavily oriented toward knowledge creation and capture based on the modern tools of AI/ML. The human value add would be a cognitive process that focused on problem identification and hypothesis development. The students from a young age would be immersed in problem identification and problem-solving, much the same way those young

6. https://sophisticatedfinance.typepad.com/sophisticated_finance/
7. https://roberthhacker.medium.com/
8. https://alpha.school/?
9. https://alpha.school/the-program/#love

lion cubs are brought up by their mothers on *Instagram*. Every living thing has been programmed by evolution to explore and then exploit. Child education needs to return to a focus on this fundamental principle. Such an approach is consistent with CAS.

Perhaps the most challenging issue is how to close the achievement gap across racial, socioeconomic, and linguistic groups. Based on my time at OLPC, I would recommend a corporate surtax by county for poor-performing locales to pay for an improved educational offering in public elementary schools. Regardless of the demographics, the children start to fall behind in pre-K and elementary school. All schools also need to have access to a high-quality Internet connection. Student evaluation would be based on graduation rates against state averages in sixth grade and a "final" state exam to graduate from high school. While such exams might be considered antithetical to self-directed and personalized learning, the highly acclaimed Finnish education system uses such an exam as the only national evaluation for high-school graduation. An interesting feature of the Finnish system is that K-12 curriculum is determined at the local city level.

Note: President Obama eased "No Child Left Behind" in 2012, leading to precipitous and continuing decline in student test scores in all grade levels, as shown below. The performance gap also widened between the highest and lowest performers as shown in Figure 5.[10]

10. https://www.the74million.org/article/interactive-see-how-student-achievement-gaps-are-growing-in-your-state/

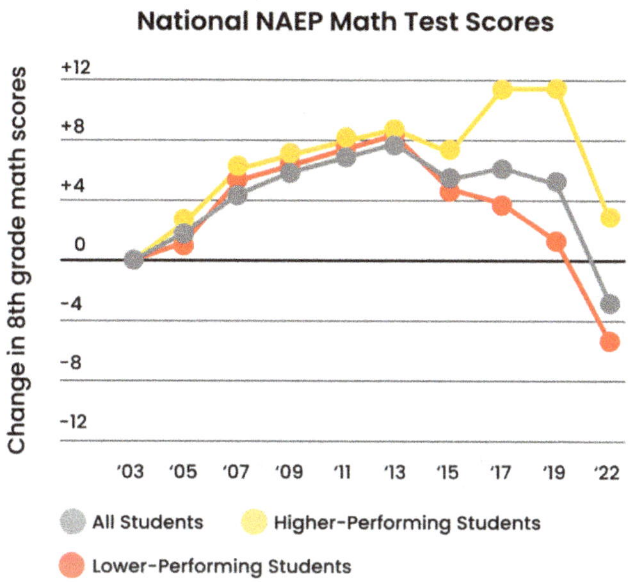

FIGURE 5. NATIONAL NAEP MATH TEST SCORES

Source: The74 Chad Aldemaan: National NAEP Math Test Scores.

An idea that I like a lot is part-time and retired people as teachers. Their stories and practical perspectives take the regimentation out of the classroom and tend to insert more practical active learning. Online classes and pre-recorded classes would provide scheduling flexibility to attract part-time and retired people. This approach would also address the teacher shortage, where former teachers now opt for better pay and shorter work hours in private sector jobs. Despite the availability of various graduate-level education degrees, in my experience, most people learn to teach in the classroom. I would support this approach by providing the teachers with a syllabus and lesson plans prepared by the school district for the formal classroom part of the day. A related issue is the increased number of school administrators with no appreciable growth in teachers (or students), as shown below. Since 2000 admin staff has increased 95%: teachers 39% and students 5%. We should transfer the school budgets from administrator salaries to more in class resources such as teaching assistants, hands on learning materials, or lab spaces.

Role	Percentage change from 2018-19 to 2021-22
School Psychologists	16.6%
LEA Administrators	13.4%
Student Support Staff	9.0%
School Administrative Support	5.7%
Guidance Counselors	1.7%
Teachers	0.2%
School Administrators	-0.7%
All Other Support Staff	-3.5%
Paraprofessionals	-4.0%
Librarians/ Media Support Staff	-4.3%
LEA Administrative Support Staff	-7.1%
Instructional Coordinators	-18.2%

FIGURE 6.

Source: National Center for Education Statistics, Common Core of Data (CCD)

Another promising approach has been developed in China. The Chinese government pre-records a national expert on a subject. These online classes are then offered nationwide. Such an approach ensures consistent higher-quality lessons and reduces the risks and problems from a shortage of quality teachers. (It also obviously reduces the problem of free speech in China.) Perhaps states could join together to create this online curriculum, which might reduce the likelihood of reduced freedom of speech in the United States.

Finland, Alpha schools, and even the Chinese approach all show examples of adaptive behavior, flexible approaches to resource use. The philosophy is both student-centric and shaped by local inputs. Maybe explicit, but for sure implicit, the various strategies also serve the greater community. All of these approaches are indicative of emergent strategy. To close with a quote from Einstein. "We can't solve today's problems with the same mentality that created them." To improve the populations "mentality" and familiarity, public education needs urgently to increase the importance, awareness, and time devoted to climate, environmental, and sustainability issues. We discuss environment in Chapter 11.

10

The Future: Medicine, Healthcare, and Health?

> "There are myriad opportunities to improve the way healthcare systems run, the way patients interact with the healthcare system, and how we can comprehend and make use of the massive amounts of data that are generated."
>
> —Andrew Naidech, MD. Northwestern Medicine

THE CURRENT SITUATION

While many would tout the advances in medicine and healthcare since WW II, I would point out that the complexity of the current situation is unmatched in human history. Lifespan is increasing with several commentators anticipating a human lifespan of 100+ years. With increased lifespan will come the need for larger personal and government budgets for healthcare. Environmental issues, such as air and water quality, are increasing, which will have a negative impact on human health. Lastly, the world is more connected by air transportation and global supply chains, which COVID-19 demonstrated can speed up the spread of epidemics and related catastrophic events. This limited analysis points out that much of the complexity in healthcare is based in the local domain, which explains in part my focus on healthcare as an issue for subnational, more local governments. *After water quality and water supply, I think there is no more important local issue than healthcare.*

Weening local government off their reliance on federal government "leadership" in healthcare might be a daunting task, but that may be the problem. Healthcare is heavily reliant currently on an inflexible, non-adaptive government. We must also recognize that the payor near monopoly in insurance permits more focus on profitability than health outcomes. And perhaps the most disorganized "public" information system is electronic health records—EHR—that has proven to be resistant to digital transformation.

Medical research and new drug approval should be done by the NSF (at the federal level) in order to better achieve economies of scale and reduce the risk of siloed information. Such an organization would be modeled on the National Academies of Sciences, Engineering, and Medicine (NASEM), an independent, trusted adviser to the NSF and other federal agencies.

I believe that healthcare should be a subnational government responsibility. Such an approach allows for better matching to a community's values, ethics, local priorities, and environmental challenges. The well-being of the local economy might argue against such an approach focused at the city or county level. However, that is why we have the concept of priorities. Each county could decide what they want to put ahead of healthcare or elementary education or law enforcement or the environment. Not easy questions, but these tough decisions will increasingly become urgent local priorities. As the environment becomes a bigger and bigger healthcare issue, I think it logical for healthcare to become increasingly local. The impact of the degrading environment on public health is underappreciated, especially when we consider the impact on food supply, water management, air quality, and catastrophic events. Increased local taxes would reflect the local priorities for services. A critical challenge will be for government at the city or state level to take advantage of digital transformation to reduce overhead expenses and staffing costs.

The number of Americans aged 65 and older is projected to increase from 58 million in 2022 to 82 million by 2050 (a 41% increase), and the 65-and-older age group's share of the total population is projected to rise from 17% to 23%.[1,2] The poverty rate for Americans ages 65 and older has dropped sharply during the past ~60 years, from nearly 30% in 1966 to 10% (2023),[3] suggesting a better ability for the elders to manage their healthcare. However, much of the funding for their healthcare will come from Medicare. By 2050, Medicare spending alone is projected to exceed 5% of GDP, up from 3.2% today. Such a level of spending strongly suggests the need for increases in taxes, higher copay amounts, separate insurances for routine medical care, and surgeries or all of the above. Another alternative would be increased use of generic drugs and more fixed payment approaches for annual healthcare such as value-based care, comprehensive primary care, or capitation. Many of the developed countries in Europe provide equal or better healthcare at significantly lower cost per patient compared with the United States, as I described in Chapter 8. Cost reduction in the provision of medical care is long overdue. Increasing use of robotic technology for routine medical care and surgeries, better early disease detection through advanced testing and better education on personal health management may each lower medical costs for everyone, including the elders.

In this chapter, I discuss the future of:

- Medical Research
- The State of Medical Diagnosis and Therapies
- The Social Determinants of Health (SDOH).

1. U.S. Census Bureau. 2023. 2023 National Population Projections Tables: Main Series. https://www.census.gov/data/tables/2023/demo/popproj/2023-summary-tables.html
2. https://www.prb.org/resources/fact-sheet-aging-in-the-united-states/
3. Emily A. Schrider and John Creamer. 2023, September 12. "Poverty in the United States: 2022," Table A-1. People in Poverty by Selected Characteristics: 2021 and 2022 (Report no. P60-280), U.S. Census Bureau. https://www.census.gov/data/tables/2023/demo/income-poverty/p60-280.html

MEDICAL RESEARCH

I believe that biology and medical science will be the research focus for the twenty-first century. The suitability of AI/ML to analyze and predict is based on the component make up of every natural system starting at the atom, molecule, and cellular levels, which lends itself to applications for better medicine and healthcare. I will focus here on the four megatrends in medicine and healthcare research. All four trends are heavily reliant on AI/ML and digital technologies. Each of these four megatrends can be broken down at many levels of study to include 1) Precision medicine and genomics, 2) Multi-Omics, 3) Crispr and gene editing, 4) Systems biology, 5) Applied AI/ML (stem cells, etc.), 6) Spatial Transcriptomics, 7) Immunotherapy, 8) Neuroscience and brain research, 9) Environmental health, 10) Regenerative medicine, 11) Robotics, 12) Mental health. This level of analysis would require its own book and others who are more qualified to write it.

The four megatrends are:

1. AI and ML. Image analysis for biomarkers and other evidences of disease using AI/ML is advancing rapidly, particularly in the most problematic areas of cardio, cancer, and neuroscience. The biggest challenge may be in securing insurance reimbursement given that early diagnosis may not yet be paired with effective early treatment plans. The use of multimodal data for early disease detection is another promising application of AI/ML, particularly as increased attention is being paid to creating more and more medical research databases. Using generative AI also shows particular promise to counsel patients for mental health and disability issues. In several areas of applied generative AI, research shows the algorithms alone do better diagnosis than the doctor alone or the doctor combined with the generative AI. The entire field of precision medicine, medicine designed for an individual patient, is an exciting area of research using AI/ML. The list of examples will only get longer with time.

2. Digital health and remote care. This approach encompasses technologies, such as telemedicine, wearable devices, remote patient monitoring, and digital therapeutics. The increasing popularity of these approaches will increase with each new generation's confidence in digital solutions, their knowledge of life styles for better health, and as the AI/ML advances to better incorporate multimodal data. The increasing expectation for real-time customer experience in every facet of modern life also supports the movement toward remote digital health, with the devices already capable to request emergency services with no human decision-making.
3. Genomics and Precision Medicine. Genomics is the comprehensive study of an organism's entire genome, all its genes, and their interactions with each other and the environment. Genomics focuses on the structure, function, evolution, and mapping of genomes, as well as analyzing the complete set of DNA within an organism. This science will eventually permit for the genomics of an individual to guide pharmacogenomics to predict individual drug responses and serve as the basis for personalized therapeutics development. Combining advances in genomics, big data analytics, and AI/ML should improve patient outcomes and potentially reduce healthcare costs. Again, the question will be how medical insurers see the economic consequences of this new medical science and how many years of patient data will be required to provide the analytical basis to the insurers for a change in therapies and treatment.
4. Health. The World Health Organization defined health in 1948 as "a state of complete physical, mental, and social well-being," moving the focus from disease to a more holistic approach to overall patient well-being.[4] Increasingly, the focus on health involves proactively preventing diseases, prolonging life, and promoting health through organized efforts and informed collective choices. Such an approach, in my view, suggests the need for increased emphasis on locale as a major determinant of health. A more holistic approach also supports additional resources for mental and psychological well-being, dementia, and other age-related emotional and psychological impairments.

---

4. World Health Organization. 1958. *The First Ten Years of the World Health Organization*. Geneva: WHO. ISBN 9789241560146.

THE STATE OF MEDICAL DIAGNOSIS AND THERAPIES

Advances in biopharma medical diagnosis and therapies, according to PitchBook,[5] are termed as mature, advanced, and emerging modalities. Mature modalities are in widespread use by doctors, hospitals, and clinics. Advanced modalities have reached "late stage clinical trials or market entry." Typically emerging modalities are at best in FDA Phase I clinical trials. The advantage to using PitchBook's venture capital oriented framework is that all of companies and their diagnostic approaches and therapies are purposefully managed to go-to-market and improve people's lives and not likely to be "science for science's sake."

"The [advanced] modalities include cell therapies, gene therapies, nucleic acid-based treatments, drug conjugates, and gene editing. By leveraging advances in molecular biology, these approaches target diseases at their genetic and cellular roots, offering the promise of precision medicine and improved patient outcomes."[6] Many of these modalities offer the possibility to become platforms where the therapeutic functionality can be applied across a wide range of diseases rather than the more traditional single disease focus. The similarities of this approach to info-centric platform computing should be apparent to the reader.

Emerging modalities, according to PitchBook, include Microbiome and Phage, Oncolytic Viruses, and Tissue and Biomaterials. Microbiome studies of gut bacteria have advanced to the point where databases are being created. A project at the University of Chicago assembled 160,000 gut microbiome samples and applied a consistent sequencing methodology across all samples.[7] Antibiotic-resistant infections are in large part driving Phage Therapy, which uses viruses to target and treat bacterial infections. Clinical trials are expected to increase in 2025, but limited clinical trials began as early as 2022. Oncolytic viruses are a promising form of can-

5. https://files.pitchbook.com/website/files/pdf/2025_Biopharma_Modalities_VC_Ecosystem_Overview_Preview.pdf

6. Ibid.

7. https://biologicalsciences.uchicago.edu/news/gut-microbiome-data-underscores-gaps-global-representation

cer immunotherapy that selectively infect and destroy cancer cells. Oncolytic viruses activate the immune system against tumor cells. The pace of clinical trials is expected to increase in 2025. Tissue and biomaterials use advances in materials science to engineer and create platforms to treat medical conditions. Advanced imaging technologies, such as MRI and CT scans, are used in tissue and internal organ diagnosis. Tissue engineering uses biomaterials as scaffolds to repair or replace damaged tissues like skin, bone, and cartilage. Clinical trials are predominantly focused on ophthalmology, dentistry, and vascular medicine.[8]

Beyond the scope of biopharma, medical devices, and medical imaging show much promise to advance diagnostic methods and therapy. Applications in oncology are the top area for therapeutics. Neurology is making use of new functionality in MRI and echocardiography is being used in clinical trials for cardiac imaging. All of these examples and many more are in clinical trials in the United States. The development of new devices and imaging methods will largely focus on cardiology, oncology, and neurology.

SOCIAL DETERMINANTS OF HEALTH

I am not a social liberal. I think that in many ways, the United States and Europe are trying to legislate what are personal decisions. But, in 2025, in the United States, we provide inadequate support to the socially and economically disadvantaged, especially in the areas of education and healthcare. And, we will never properly address the healthcare issues until we improve the concurrent problem of education for the disadvantaged. Nobel economist Michael Spence showed in his book, *The Next Convergence*, that poverty is caused by an asymmetry of information. The disadvantaged lacked the information to protect their self-interests, which in large part is due to a lack of education and the related inability to secure better information. Piaget's quote, "only education is capable of saving our societies

8. https://pmc.ncbi.nlm.nih.gov/articles/PMC466960/

…" is grounded in the ability of education to address any asymmetry. This same asymmetry of information explains many of the issues in healthcare for the disadvantaged.

The concept of SDOH is traced back to a World Health Organization (WHO) initiative that began in 2003. By 2008, WHO was focused on SDOH as a matter of social justice. By 2018, WHO had arrived at a more holistic view, "social determinants of health are the conditions in which people are born, grow, live, work and age."[9] Kaiser Family Foundation (KFF) includes in the SDOH definition "the factors of socioeconomic status, education, neighborhood and physical environment, employment, and social support networks, as well as access to health care." I commend KFF for explicitly, including education, as shown in Figure 7.

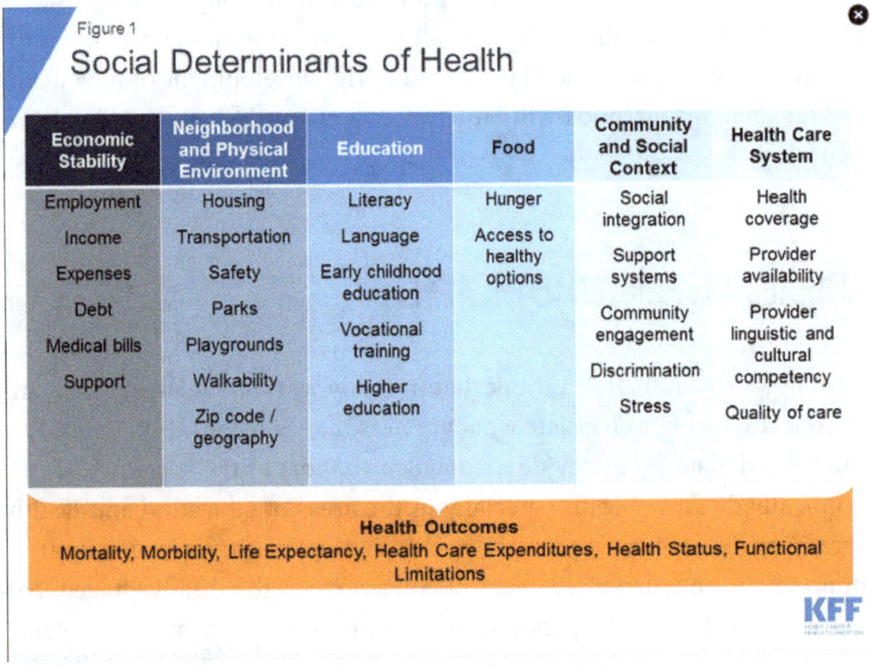

FIGURE 7. SOCIAL DETERMINANTS OF HEALTH

Source: KFF. (2019, May 18). Beyond healthcare. https://www.kff.org/report-section/beyond-health-care-the-role-of-social-determinants-in-promoting-health-and-health-equity-issue-brief/

9. "About Social Determinants of Health," World Health Organization, accessed April 25, 2018. http://www.who.int/social_determinants/sdh_definition/en/

In 2010, President Obama signed the Affordable Care Act (ACA) into law. In 2016, the Center for Medicare and Medicaid Innovation (CMMI) was established under ACA. These programs funded state initiatives in population health focused on disadvantaged communities. The focus at the state and community level is consistent with what I propose for better healthcare, but the actual results of these federal programs were mixed at best. Some cost savings were achieved but typically below forecasted levels and the more important metric of improved health outcomes were frequently not achieved. The failing I think was in the approach.

The Rockefeller Foundation has pioneered the development of social programs since its founding in 1913. Equally important is the foundation's pioneering thinking in strategic philanthropy. Over the years, their analysis showed that projects assumed a linear, causal logic that overlooked the multifaceted reality explained by complexity science. "These problems are dynamic, nonlinear, and counter-intuitive. They are the result of the interplay between multiple independent factors that influence each other in ever-changing ways."[10] In 2008, the foundation adopted an approach called "emergent strategy," which is explained below:

> an emergent approach, co-creating its initial strategy with dozens of other organizations, strengthening the global ecosystem that determined the outcomes they sought, and continuously modifying its strategy as the staff sensed opportunities to amplify positive developments along the way.[11]

Such an approach is matched to the organizations involved in a project, their particular expertise, and budget availability. Many academics have criticized emergent strategy, stating that it lacks adaptability to local conditions. I would refer these academics to the foundational writings on CAS by the thinkers at SFI. Adaptability is a foundational concept in complexity. The likely reason for the academic conclusions is more likely inadequate instruction in the values and philosophy of complexity to a project's leadership. In fairness to the academics, we should recognize Professor Henry

10. https://ssir.org/up_for_debate/article/strategic_philanthropy#
11. Ibid.

Mintzberg's seminal thinking on emergent strategy. "Emergent strategy accepts that a realized strategy emerges over time as the initial intentions collide with, and accommodate to, a changing reality. The term 'emergent' implies that an organization is learning what works in practice."[12] Mintzberg, the Rockefeller Foundation, and I look like we all agree.

To close, I would recommend emergent strategies to address SDOH. I would point out that such an approach is rarely used by government, the NASA project to put a man on the moon a notable exception. No one organization has all the knowledge and experience to properly address an issue in the SDOH or any other social problem. An ecosystem style approach, consistent with emergent strategy, would combine government, private sector organizations, academia (and NGOs) to more effectively expand the available skill set and experience, provided the heavy hand of a federal government does not dictate or bury the team in bureaucratic reporting to no real purpose.

In the next chapter, I discuss the environment, which will have far-reaching consequences in the twenty-first century and in particular for the potential impact on human health and healthcare.

12. Ibid.

11

The Environmental Challenge: A Case Study in Complexity

"Since living systems at all levels are networks, we must visualize the web of life as living systems (networks) interacting in network fashion with other systems (networks)."

—Fritjof Capra, Pier Luigi Luisi, The Systems View of Life)

THE CURRENT SITUATION

I would hope for environmental science to rival biology and medical science in terms of research funding in the twenty-first century, but I am doubtful. We have made so little progress on the environment. When the Berlin Wall fell in 1989, President George HW Bush had the chance to define a new national vision around the environment. Neither he nor any subsequent president has had the foresight to see the importance of the environment or any other theme as a new vision for the United States. For example, the U.S. federal government budgeted total environmental spending of approximately US$150B or 0.54% of GDP for FY 2025.[1] In comparison, the European Union (EU) committed approximately €130B or 0.8% of their GDP in

1. https://fiscaldata.treasury.gov/americas-finance-guide/federal-spending/

2022.[2] Just matching the EU GDP percentage would have added approximately US$72B in additional U.S. government funding … annually!!

It is the scale of the need, the spending for environmental research, infrastructure, conservation, and remediation that prompts me to propose a centralized federal government department responsible for climate and sustainability, food, water, agriculture, weather, and natural resource conservation. Ten percent or more of the new department's budget should be just for research in government and university labs, which would represent approximately US$22B in my expanded total environment budget of US$222B (150+72). Current spending for environmental research in the United States is only US$4.5B in FY 2025[3] spread across several government units. The urgency and complexity of the environmental problem necessitates the increased spending.

Much like the entire federal government, the Environmental Protection Agency (EPA), established in 1970, needs to be reorganized and a new strategy drafted. The chart of temperature since 1950, shown below, might support my conclusion. The original EPA mandate reflected the very limited understanding of the issues at the time and a primary focus on regulation and enforcement. Interestingly, almost 50% of the EPA budget goes for grants to local governments, universities, and nonprofit foundations. The scale of this funding supports my view that more current federal responsibility and funding should be at the subnational level. I have elected to leave the department responsible for the environment at the national level. Increasingly I expect environmental problems to be multi-state problems. Sea-level rise, CO_2 levels, and air pollution support my view.

2. https://ec.europa.eu/eurostat/statistics-explained/index.php?title=Government_expenditure_on_environmental_protection
3. https://bidenwhitehouse.archives.gov/briefing-room/statements-releases/2024/03/11/fact-sheet-the-presidents-budget-creates-good-paying-clean-jobs-cuts-energy-costs-and-delivers-on-the-presidents-ambitious-climate-agenda/#:~:text=The%20Budget%20includes%20$4.5%20billion%20for%20climate,Atmospheric%20Administration%20(NOAA)%2C%20NSF%2C%20and%20other%20agencies.&text=The%20Budget%20builds%20on%20historic%20international%20climate,billion%20represent%20a%20near%2Dsixfold%20increase%20from%202021

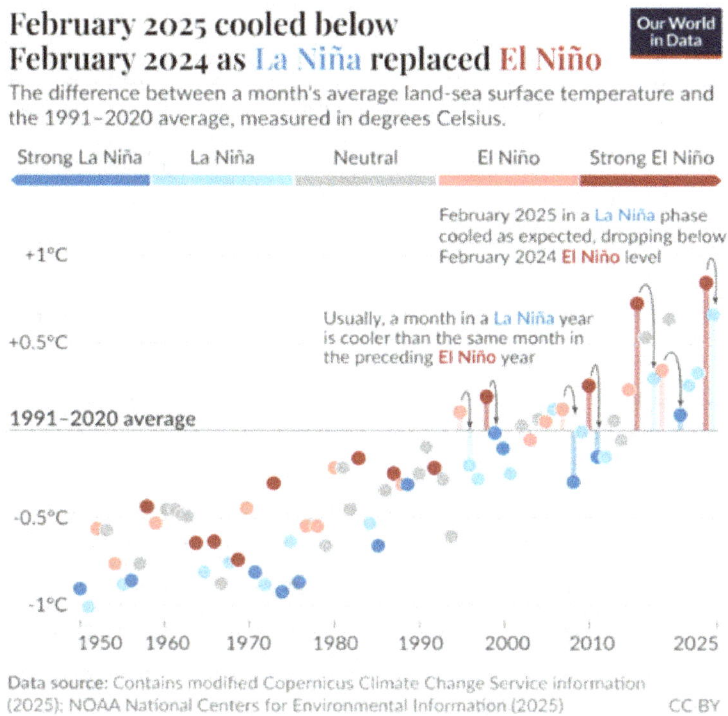

FIGURE 8.

Another way to look at the problem is in terms of the market, but who is the customer for the better environmental solutions? Who purchases a product to reduce CO_2 or to remediate a wetlands situation. A small part of the solution can be provided by consumers buying Tesla cars or using solar panels in their homes, but these measures barely move the needle. For example, "Just 100 companies have been the source of more than 70% of the world's greenhouse gas emissions since 1988" and "more than half of global industrial emissions since 1988 … can be traced to just 25 corporate and state-owned entities."[4] To achieve scale of impact, we need the behavior of the big corporates and the federal government to change and

4. https://www.theguardian.com/sustainable-business/2017/jul/10/100-fossil-fuel-companies-investors-responsible-71-global-emissions-cdp-study-climate-change

their perspective and the perspective of universities are all different. I think we need a new form of multi-stakeholder collaboration and partnership involving the large corporations, the federal and subnational governments, academia, foundations, and even the NGOs. Such a collection of participants is another application of "ecosystem." Such an approach provides the model for the adaptive, collaborative, and networked features of CAS and more importantly to succeed in the increasingly complex and uncertain twenty-first century. This ecosystem approach is also my proposed solution to the equally challenging issue of Energy, which I discuss in the next chapter. Of course, the two issues—the environment and energy—are closely related, and a similar solution should perhaps not be surprising.

At the risk of future draconian federal laws and regulation to address continued environmental decline, the ecosystem participants must come together as soon as possible to first define the values and principles and then the objectives, tangible metrics, and timeline. At that point a budget could be established. With the advances in quantitative methods, an agent-based model or a digital twin model could be used to refine the results. Absent the modeling, WW II and the Apollo project to put a man on the moon might be examples of such an ecosystem approach. While these projects were both government led, today I think we need someone like Eric Schmidt, former Google CEO, Mark Benioff, founder of Salesforce and visionary investor in the Singapore ecosystem, or Daphne Kohler, MacArthur scholar and cofounder of Coursera and other technology startups. Such a project will not succeed without the corporate perspective being recognized and the re-election issues such as job creation being de minimis. These candidates and others have the multidisciplinary experience to successfully operate at the national level in such a diverse context. Based on my own experience moving from the corporate world to a state university, I think it is more effective when the corporate executive transitions to head such a project rather than an academic or government official. Recognizing the idealism of this proposal, the problems today share a complexity and criticality that calls for a new approach to problem-solving and a modern operating style. More on this theme in Chapter 15. To implement such an approach demonstrates the urgent need to redesign the government to immediately address the impending environmental crisis.

THE ISSUE(S)

The earth is a fixed biosphere with complex physical and adaptive systems that contends with the constant interaction between manmade and natural systems. The situation is further complicated by the scientific reductionism of Descartes that shaped science beginning in the seventeenth century. Such an approach did not foster a holistic view but rather led to man considering everything as simply a component or resource to be used (and exploited). This view supported increasing industrialization and urbanization, but the cost of such narrow-mindedness is coming to a head with the impending environmental problems.

There is widespread agreement, despite vocal and powerful minority opinions, that the major environmental issues require immediate attention, more research funding, and commercialization of the solutions to reach the scale of impact required. The major issues and simple definitions and examples are listed below.

- Climate change and decarbonization
  Addresses corporate emissions reduction, CO_2 removal, the results of natural carbon sinks, and global warming and the related effects such as the melting polar ice caps and seal level rise

- Food, water, and sustainable agriculture
  Considers drought, changing rainfall levels, resistant crop development, land quality, innovative farming practices, and consideration of the international food supply chain.

- Renewable energy and other technologies
  Technologically advancing solar, wind, hydropower, battery technologies, and the development of nuclear power and fission.

- Sustainable materials
  Development of biodegradable, renewable, recyclable, and sustainable materials and products and advancing the state of the art in advanced manufacturing.

- Bioremediation
  Using bioventing, biosparging, natural attenuation, composting, biopiles, waste water treatment, and biohazard remediation.

- Climate Adaptation and Resilience
  Risk minimization from extreme weather events, climate change, and changing ecosystems and related infrastructure considerations.

This list is intended to be comprehensive but not complete. Remember the natural and manmade systems are changing on a daily basis.

Environmental data and analytics is an increasingly important research and commercialization focus. AI/ML are being used to gather and analyze multimodal environmental data to improve models and forecasting tools to inform decision-making and policy on a timely basis. One example is CEJST (Executive Order 14008, Tackling the Climate Crisis at Home and Abroad § 222[a], 86 F.R. 7619, 7631 [Jan. 27, 2021]), a federal geospatial mapping tool that identifies locations faced with significant burdens caused by environmental factors. An earlier example is Munich Re, the world's largest reinsurance company. They began climate modeling in 1970, decades before their insurance peers and almost everybody. "This move established the company as a leader in climate risk modeling, driving its business success when the issue of climate change became more widely appreciated."[5]

Perhaps not since the Chernobyl disaster or COVID-19 have humans been reminded of existential risk. The expectation of new "Force 6" hurricanes in Florida and the southeast United States increases my concerns about existential environmental risk. Every time you read about an entire civi-

5. Jeremy Rifkin, *The Third Industrial Revolution.*

lization that disappeared, the cause is always man's stupidity, the environment or both. Some days the moon or Mars looks like a viable alternative. Alternatively, we can hope the startup community has a favorable impact. According to Sightline Climate, "since 2020, about 3,900 climate tech companies have raised over $182 billion in venture funding."[6] Alternatively, in March 2025, France announced that they are planning for a 4C (7.2F) temperature rise by the end of the century.[7] Views on the environment are very mixed, with the French government apparently not anticipating much progress over the next ~75 years. The energy outlook is a key consideration in forecasting the environment, which we discuss in the next chapter.

Note: As an aside, I am increasingly coming to the conclusion that the finance industry, including financial institutions like Munich Re, is the leading industry to adopt new AI/ML and computational methods. Such technology is used to manage trading and operating risk, product development, and customer experience. These institutions have the advantage of an info-centric product that lends itself to digital transformation and have always had to operate in a real-time, digital transaction environment. Perhaps John Reed, former Chairman of Citibank, modernized digital banking in the 1980s, informed by his time at SFI where he was a major benefactor.

6. https://www.ctvc.co/30bn-and-14-fall-as-market-finds-new-normal-in-24/
7. https://www.rfi.fr/en/environment/20250310-france-rolls-out-plan-to-prepare-for-4c-temperature-rise-by-end-of-century-climate-change

12

The Future: It's All About Energy

> "This is our biological metabolic rate living as naturally evolved animals. As social animals now living in cities we still need just a lightbulb equivalent of food to stay alive but, in addition, we now require homes, heating, lighting, automobiles, roads, airplanes, computers, and so on. Consequently, the amount of energy needed to support an average person living in the United States has risen to an astounding 11,000 watts. This social metabolic rate is equivalent to the entire needs of about a dozen elephants. Furthermore, in making this transition from the biological to the social our overall population has increased from just a few million to more than seven billion. No wonder there's a looming energy and resource crisis."
>
> —Geoffrey West, Scale

John Wheeler showed us that epistemological and metaphysical reality can be understood in terms of information. Matter stores the information. Matter takes up space and has mass. Einstein showed us that there is an energy–mass equivalence, $E=mc^2$. In summary, reality can be explained in terms of information and energy. Perhaps not by coincidence, AI/ML is sensitive to and reliant upon both the inputs of information and energy.

THE CURRENT SITUATION

When we consider energy, paramount today is electricity usage. We need to consider generative AI, cloud computing, data centers, energy storage, and the national and local electricity grids. Electric vehicles and the new Fourth Industrial Revolution technologies, such as enhanced audio and video usage, advanced manufacturing, and real-time sensors, are all big users of electricity. The Electric Power Research Institute (EPRI) forecasts that data centers alone could grow from 4% today to 9+% of electricity usage by 2030, or as much as 675 TWh. Such rapid growth makes clear the need for greater efficiency in electricity usage through improved technology, better modeling tools to ensure grid availability and reliability, and more collaboration between the governments, the utilities, the data center operators, and other large industrial users.[1]

To put the numbers in perspective, "ChatGPT processes billions of prompts per year and consumes a whopping 226.8 GWh of energy annually. That's enough to fully charge about 3.13 million electric vehicles (95% of electric cars in the 2023)" or provide the daily electricity usage of Belgium[2] and the environmental impact does not stop there. For example, ChatGPT uses over 19 million gallons of water daily. And, the industry may need up to 8× more energy storage or an addition of 2,000 GW by 2030, according to UBS. With 59% of energy generation to be intermittent renewables by 2030, storage and the necessary strategic materials become a more critical issue.[3] Required investment in the U.S. energy grid is forecasted to be US$1.4T by 2030 and the same additional amount by 2050, according to Deloitte.[4] This build-out alone has significant environmental impact. The Heathrow closure in March 2025 shows the importance of the electricity grid and its management and maintenance. Power and power outages are a function of both the supply and the reliability of the related infrastructure. As en-

1. https://www.epri.com/research/products/3002028905
2. https://balkangreenenergynews.com/chatgpt-consumes-enough-power-in-one-year-to-charge-over-three-million-electric-cars/
3. https://www.ubs.com/global/en/investment-bank/insights-and-data/2025/esg-dmc.html
4. Deloitte analysis of S&P Global Market Intelligence, "Utility capital expenditures final update for H2 2024," accessed December 23, 2024.

ergy usage continues to increase, the single point of failure that shut down Heathrow will no longer be acceptable. The multiplicity of environmental issues from increased electricity usage creates a critically complex set of operating and financial concerns that is further discussed in Chapter 14.

RENEWABLE ENERGY

In 2024, the World Resources Institute estimates renewable sources of energy to reach ~24% of total electricity generation in the United States, which was provided by:

- Wind. In 2022, wind became the largest source of renewable energy, providing 434 billion KWh. In 2024, wind accounted for 10.3% of U.S. utility-scale generating capacity.
- Solar. The fastest-growing source of renewable energy is solar, but it is an intermittent provider available only during daylight hours. In 2024, it accounted for 7%, which included 1.9% from small-scale solar PV (systems <1 MW).
- Hydropower. Water availability impacts the reliability of hydropower. Hydropower provided an estimated 6+% in 2024.[5]

Other sources of renewable energy include geothermal and biomass, which have not reached significant production levels in the U.S. Nuclear energy, while not technically a renewable, is a carbon-free energy that provided 18.6% of U.S. power generation in 2023.

Fossil fuels, which include natural glass, coal, and petroleum, accounted for 60% in 2022 and 57.9% in 2024. The U.S. Energy Information Administration (EIA) forecasts that fossil fuel power generation will decline to 44%.[6] Total power generation in 2050 is shown in Figure 9.

5. https://www.wri.org/insights/clean-energy-progress-united-states
6. https://www.eia.gov/todayinenergy/detail.php?id=51698

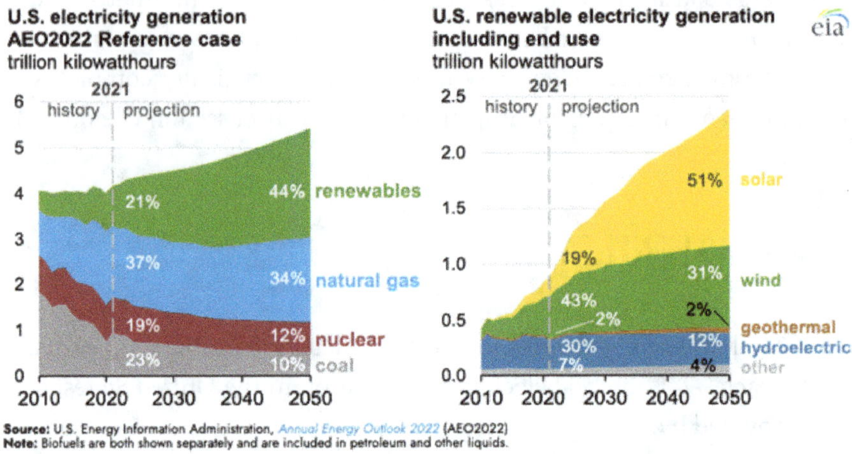

FIGURE 9.

Source: U.S. Energy Information Administration, *Annual Energy Outlook 2022* (AEO2022).
Note: Biofuels are both shown separately and are included in petroleum and other liquids.

While the growth in renewables is encouraging, the decline in nuclear energy is most troubling to me. The safety of nuclear technology has advanced significantly since Three Mile Island (1979). I live 30 miles from the Turkey Point nuclear plant. Except for an increase in the resident alligator (1976) and now crocodile populations at the plant, there has been no noticeable change in the plant risk assessment in the twenty-five years I have lived in south Florida. (This animal migration, however, does tend to indicate a declining environment in the Everglades National Park forty miles away and better conditions at the nuclear plant. Alligators have 245 million years of environmental evaluation experience and crocodiles who came later to Turkey Point have 80 million years of experience. Perhaps we could use robots to learn alligator/crocodile sounds and then ask the animals questions about environmental conditions.)

RESEARCH

Accelerating demand for electricity brought about by the growth in AI and related infrastructure and the crossover to increased use of renewable and nuclear energy to replace fossil fuel generation has prompted an increase in related research. Related environmental issues, grid resilience, and geopolitical considerations also deserve increased research, analysis, and tangible proposals. I think all of these issues tend to support the use of the ecosystem concept, which the nonprofit Electricity Power Research Institute (EPRI) uses for their projects. In October 2024, "EPRI partnered with major utilities, power companies, grid operators, and tech firms like Google, Meta, and NVIDIA to demonstrate how data centers could transition from passive energy consumers to active, flexible grid resources." "The Data Center Flexible Load Initiative (DCFlex) will establish five to ten "Flexibility Hubs" starting in 2025 to explore innovative strategies for integrating data centers into the grid, including load management, advanced cooling technologies, and clean backup power generation."[7] Maybe we should all remember that "newer concepts like ecosystems can be applied to update older projects."

Some of the additional issues that require further research and immediate attention are listed below:

1. Environmental issues. Climate change caused by increased greenhouse gases will increase global warming. The effects from global warming will melt glaciers and polar ice caps leading to sea level rise of 10–12 inches in the United States according to NOAA and other U.S. agencies.[8] Biodiversity degradation is also expected to increase as deforestation, increased CO_2 levels and air and water pollution increase.

7. https://www.powermag.com/the-big-picture-how-much-power-will-data-centers-consume-infographic/
8. https://sealevel.globalchange.gov/resources/2022-sea-level-rise-technical-report/#:~:text=2020%2D2050,in%20the%20next%2030%20years

2. Grid resilience. With increased demand for electricity, grid resilience becomes increasingly important and the use of smart grid technology becomes a priority. Use of micro-grids provides a possible alternative.
3. Energy Storage. With intermittent energy sources such as solar and wind forecasted to increase their share of electricity supply, better storage battery materials and technology will be required.
4. Geopolitical considerations. The forecast for energy indicates that the environmental issue(s) only become more global each year. With the exception of certain military action, little evidence exists for sustained global cooperation.

By the nature of the current and forecasted energy supply, we need to deploy new technologies faster, conserve resources, and better educate the global population to the increasingly urgent situation. According to McKinsey, we also need to rapidly reduce the cost of the necessary technologies and increase the deployed scale of these technologies.[9] Regardless of the perspective, the challenge will be to properly manage John Wheeler's convergence of energy and information in an environmentally responsible way to ensure the survival of mankind.

9. https://www.mckinsey.com/capabilities/sustainability/our-insights/a-radical-approach-to-cost-reduction-at-climate-tech-companies?cid=other-eml-dre-mip-mck&hlkid=d29ef18895e04399a0f201dc5d1ac0b8&hctky=10393242&hdpid=30d032d8-4f9d-4843-a73d-c192fb39b447

13

Defense: Is It 1939?

> "Beijing has the economic, military, and technological capability to challenge the international system and America's interests within it. This is happening all along the continuum of conflict—from routine statecraft, through the use of sharp power or gray-zone tactics, to the potential for sustained combat operations and an expanded and capable nuclear enterprise"
>
> —Kathleen Hicks, U.S. Deputy Defense Secretary (2024)

My introduction to politics and military confrontation began with the Cuban Missile Crisis in October 1962. In addition to the previously mentioned realization of my mortality, I was inspired to become a patriotic American and started to learn about the United States and alternative political systems. All of this was further fueled by the birthday I share with George Washington. Born right after the end of WWII, much of my early introduction to history was based on the unwanted geographic expansion of the warring Nazis. The parallels between the Nazis and the Russian communists of 1962 was an easy conclusion for my young mind. For me, the Chinese communists are a potential repeat of the Nazis and the Russians.

However, if I were the Chinese government, I might just wait another fifty years for the United States to become financially insolvent and just another harmless trading partner like France or Germany. Add to the Chinese defense budget each year to keep the financial pressure on the Americans, but wait patiently as Buddhism teaches us.

U.S. military strategy today is based in "adaptive military strategies," which refer to the ability of armed forces to continuously adjust their tactics, operations, and overall approach to meet evolving threats, environments, and adversary capabilities.[1] Adaptive military strategies recognize the need for real-time information capture and analysis, utilizing drones, sensors, and satellites as sources for the multimodal inputs. Modern adaptive strategies integrate capabilities across land, air, sea, cyber, and space domains.

AI is modernizing modern warfare from battlefield operations to supply chain management and intelligence analysis. Cybersecurity and quantum technology for secure communications are non-battlefield priorities for continuing R&D. Sponsored research arrangements allow the DOD to fund university and corporate research partners. Venture capital investment in defense tech is an emerging field promising to replace more traditional defense industry arrangements. Some analysts see venture-backed companies taking over the leadership for a new defense technology strategy(s).

The U.S. defense budget totaled US$850B in FY 2025.[2] According to JP Morgan, VC investment in defense tech totaled US$159B (2019–2023).[3] The future of the U.S. defense industry lies at the intersection of technology innovation, strategic investments, and adaptive military strategies. With advances in AI, autonomous systems, quantum computing, and cybersecurity, the industry is poised for sustained growth in †he face of evolving global challenges and the required technology.

1. https://www.cambridge.org/core/books/abs/military-adaptation-in-war/introduction/3B8FE595B983C45BD2961AC1A5C0D8B7
2. https://www.defense.gov/News/Releases/Release/Article/3703410/department-of-defense-releases-the-presidents-fiscal-year-2025-defense-budget/#:~:text=The%20Biden%2DHarris%20Administration%20submitted%20to%20Congress%20a,billion%20for%20the%20Department%20of%20Defense%20(DoD)
3. https://www.jpmorgan.com/insights/investing/investment-trends/defense-tech-innovation-and-the-role-of-startups

China's military strategy remains a regional, defensive focused approach with moderate spending of only 1.3% of GDP (US$246B, 2025),[4] compared with 3.5% in the United States and ~2% in Europe. China's approach to military technological development focuses on AI, electronic warfare, quantum technology, and modernization. China continuously aggravates territorial issues with all neighboring countries as far away as Japan, with periodic aggressive military behaviors toward Taiwan and other neighboring countries.

India budgeted US$78.8B for FY2025[5] defense spending to support an active strategy to meet China in the Indian Ocean and on the Himalayan border between the countries. Indian defense technology development includes fighter aircraft and advanced missile and missile defense systems. Japan's defense budget totaled US$55B for 2025.[6] The technology focus is long-range missiles, unmanned systems, AI, integrated air and missile defense, and cyber capabilities. Their China strategy is counterstrike capabilities, fortifying southwestern islands, and enhancing joint operations with the United States to deter threats from China and North Korea. South Korea has an annual defense budget of US$52.1B in 2025[7]. Technology development focuses on fighter jets, missile defense systems, and cybersecurity. Korea's strategy is to respond to assertiveness from China and North Korea.

The size of these budgets might suggest that military tensions are increasing. Recent remarks by U.S. Secretary of Defense Pete Hegseth in Brussels on February 12th (2025) put the world on notice:

> We're … here today to directly and unambiguously express that stark strategic realities prevent the United States of America from being primarily focused on the security of Europe … The United States faces consequential threats to our homeland. We

4. https://en.wikipedia.org/wiki/Military_budget_of_China
5. https://www.internationalaffairs.org.au/australianoutlook/how-does-chinas-rising-defence-budget-affect-india/
6. https://apnews.com/article/japan-defense-budget-china-missile-drones-ba6341c527f5044b-6b5a749b6bdf0229
7. https://www.defensenews.com/global/asia-pacific/2023/12/13/south-korea-to-increase-defense-spending-over-five-years/

> must—and we are—focusing on security of our own borders … We also face a peer competitor in the Communist Chinese with the capability and intent to threaten our homeland and core national interests in the Indo-Pacific. The U.S. is prioritizing deterring war with China in the Pacific, recognizing the reality of scarcity, and making the resourcing tradeoffs to ensure deterrence does not fail … Deterrence cannot fail, for all of our sakes … As the United States prioritizes its attention to these threats, European allies must lead from the front … Together, we can establish a division of labor that maximizes our comparative advantages in Europe and Pacific respectively.

I appreciate the clarity and the commitment. Now I will worry about the next administration's philosophy and strategy. I agree that the Europeans should shoulder their fair share of the defense burden, particularly as long as Putin remains in power in Russia.

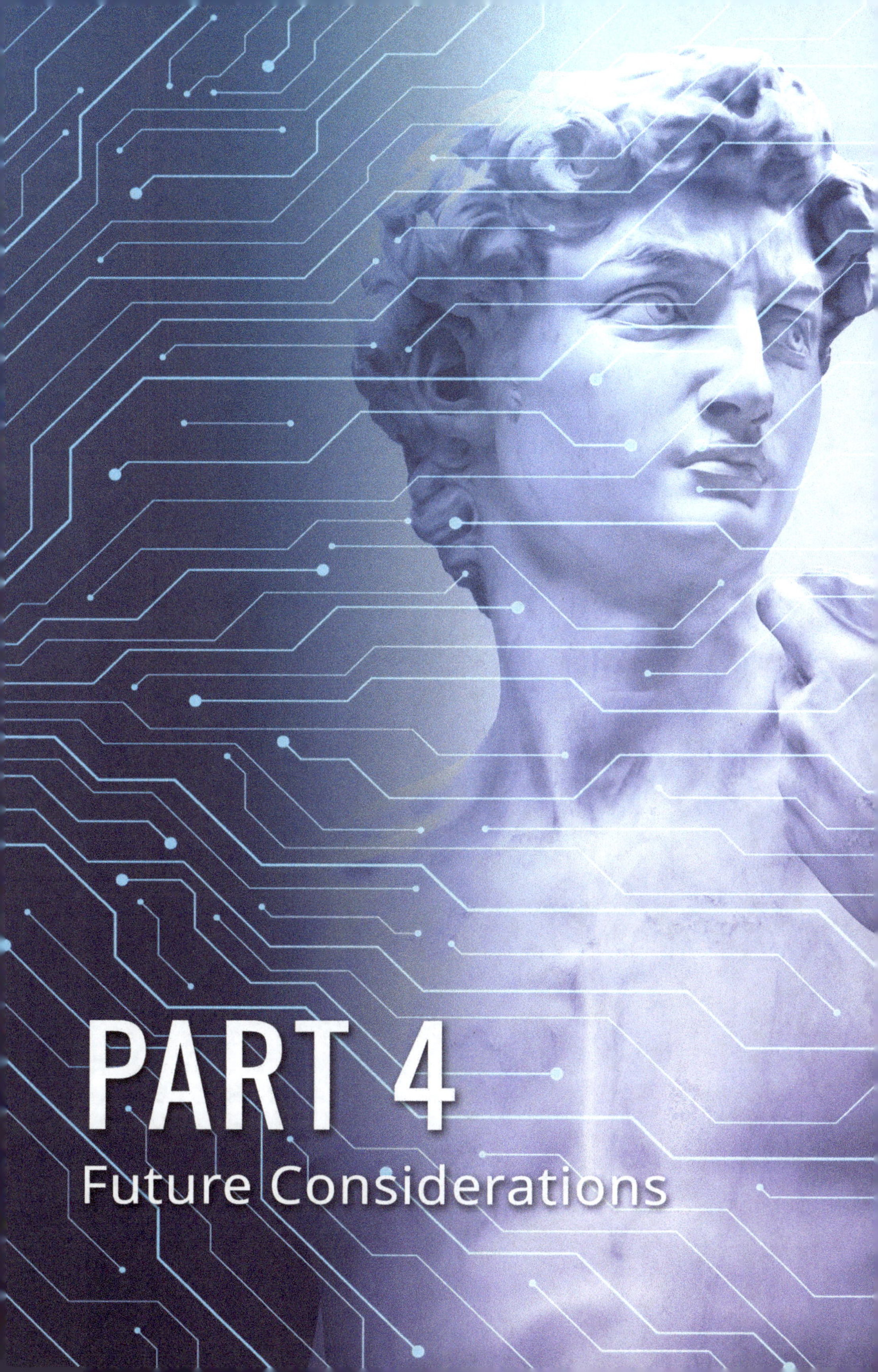

PART 4

Future Considerations

14

Risk: Things Are Not the Same

"We made the world we're living in and we have to make it over."

—James Baldwin

I realized my own inevitable mortality in 1962 during the Cuban Missile Crisis. I visited my first nuclear power plant in Oswego, NY, Nine Mile Point, in 1969 even before it started operating in 1970. I cheered in 1989 when the Berlin Wall came down. I joined the U.S. Coast Guard Auxiliary in 2002 after the 9/11 attacks, hoping to make some small contribution to national defense. The Asian Financial Crisis of 1997, when I had to evacuate Jakarta, Indonesia, showed me firsthand the inhumanity of man. These are some of the events that shaped my life and explain my thinking on risk, government and the future.

RISK

The noted economist Frank Knight defined risk as the presence of sufficient information to determine the probability (likelihood) of an event. He defined uncertainty as the lack of sufficient information to determine risk. The objective of each determination is to assess the ability to control. If we look at a simple definition of AI as "pattern recognition combined with probability," one realizes that AI is probably our most advanced tool for risk assessment. Given the complexity, uncertainty, vast amounts of networked information, unprecedented available capital and increasing number of sophisticated bad actors, AI is emerging as Bryan Arthur predicted:

> Needs drive the evolution of technology every bit as much as the possibilities for fresh combination and the unearthing of phenomena.[1]

Need is the key driver of technology development and we need AI and its advances in part to better manage the current and impending risks.

Martini and Vespasiano (2015, p. 79–85) show us the necessary key resource to manage risk. "Knowledge represents the key to success in sustainable development." In other words, it is increasingly (confirmed) that nation-states that focus on the progress of society, on greater competitiveness of the economy, and on a better and sustainable quality of life, must apply the resource of knowledge. In this way, the knowledge resource is transformed into the "most fundamental resource" (Lundvall, 1992, p. 1). John Wheeler would have agreed.

THE FOUR RISKS THAT WILL SHAPE THE UNITED STATES

There are four risk factors the United States must successfully manage to continue as a world leader.

1. Environmental Crisis. Northern Virginia, part of the metropolitan Washington, D.C. area, is the biggest data center cluster in the United States.[2] Data centers are heavy users of electricity, as discussed ear-

1. W. Bryan Arthur. 2011. The Nature of Technology: What It Is and How It Evolves. Free Press.
2. https://www.exponentialview.co/p/the-state-of-decarbonization-in-five?r=qp6q&utm_medium=ios&triedRedirect=true

lier. With this phenomenon staring them in the face, the executive branch and legislative representatives still cannot address the problem of the 2050 deadline for the environment. We have known about this deadline since the 1970s; it has not changed in 50+ years, and yet we cannot give a funding priority to accelerate the needed environmental safeguards.

In March 1972, the *Limits to Growth* was published. Under the authorship of MIT Research Fellow and systems thinking proponent Donella Meadows, the book made the following points:

1. National policies that existed prior to and in 1972 promoted exponential growth in population and material consumption.
2. There are limits to growth because Earth is finite.
3. Exponential growth on a finite planet will inevitably stop either voluntarily or due to mounting global pressures.
4. The sooner we act to slow down exponential growth and stop growth in population and material consumption, the more possibilities will be available for future generations.[3]

I think that the only way to address the environmental issues is to actively engage the private sector corporations more aggressively in the problem. Perhaps we make any operating income from new products addressing environmental issues tax free for ten years. We are not getting any tax revenue from those sources today, so what do we lose. The single most effective way for companies to scale climate technology is to aim for cost parity with carbon-intensive alternatives.[4]

2. Energy. "… The energy laws governing nature mean that an economy that demands never-ending growth will eventually hit resource limits. This is the central argument made in *Limits to Growth*, which argued that if population, resource use, and pollution kept increasing on our finite planet, eventually, economies would face environmental limits

3. https://www.issuesofsustainability.org/helpndoc-content/ClubofRomeLimitstoGrowth1972.html
4. https://www.mckinsey.com/capabilities/sustainability/our-insights/a-radical-approach-to-cost-reduction-at-climate-tech-companies?cid=other-eml-dre-mip-mck&hlkid=d29ef18895e04399a0f201dc5d1ac0b8&hctky=10393242&hdpid=30d032d8-4f9d-4843-a73d-c192fb39b447

to growth, precipitating collapse sometime in the twenty-first century.[5] Geoffrey West writing in his book *Scale* estimates that the average person living in the United States today requires 11,000 watts. Multiplying this need by the eight billion people living in the world today and "the energy and resource crisis" is both imminent and unmanageable. Better information availability makes everyone aware of the possible higher living standards, which fuels the need for more development and energy consumption and only makes the problem(s) worse.

To satisfy this need for energy both the United States and China are investing heavily in nuclear power as a low carbon emission energy source. The United States could increase current capacity from 97GW[6] to 132 GW[7] by 2035. China has current nuclear capacity of 57 GW[8] and a target to reach 100 GW[9] by 2030. I have more confidence in the forecast for China given the more favorable and quicker regulatory review process. I think the United States needs to focus on developing multiple size nuclear power plants that can service everything from a commercial data center to large communities and modern cities. If we do not implement environmentally favorable energy sources such as nuclear energy, we will never manage to reach sustainable living standards.

3. China. China policy under current President Xi Jiang has changed significantly from the successful collaborative and economically focused policies shaped by Deng Shao Ping in the 1980s. The Asia Society characterizes Xi's management style as a "highly centralized, personalized, and ideological authoritarian system" that shapes all policy decisions.[10] While successfully consolidating political power, Xi has also

---

5. https://open.substack.com/pub/exponentialview/p/the-state-of-decarbonization-in-five?r=qp6q&utm_medium=ios
6. https://en.wikipedia.org/wiki/Nuclear_power_in_the_United_States
7. https://www.utilitydive.com/news/biden-administration-plan-to-triple-us-nuclear-energy-capacity-by-2050/732807/
8. https://en.wikipedia.org/wiki/Nuclear_power_in_China
9. https://www.carbonbrief.org/qa-how-china-is-using-nuclear-power-to-reduce-its-carbon-emissions/
10. https://asiasociety.org/center-us-china-relations/chinas-new-direction-challenges-and-opportunities-us-policy

implemented a "dual circulation" strategy that emphasizes domestic consumption and innovation while balancing aggressive and collaborative international engagement. A stated objective is for China to achieve technological self-reliance. Investment in research to support this objective was reportedly more than the European Union and totaled ~US$496.3B (2023), 2.68% of GDP.[11]

The relationship between security and development remains central to China's strategic thinking. Accordingly, China pursues both economic engagement and military modernization simultaneously, seeing them as complementary rather than contradictory. China has become increasingly assertive in territorial disputes particularly with other countries bordering the South China Sea and with India. These activities are an increasing concern to Japan, Korea, India, and other countries including the United States. Consequently, all of these countries are in some stage of rearmament to meet the China threat.

A U.S. focus on a balance between security and economic development, and a reduction in expensive, pointless wars might provide the basis for a more collaborative relationship with China. China will never reach the potential its scale suggests as long as it remains a communist dictatorship. Even with a population of 1+ billion, the individual freedoms and incentives do not exist in China to achieve results consistent with the countries scale. The reportedly serious study of Singapore's success by Chinese government officials should give the United States pause. It might be said that Singapore has solved the riddle successfully of a non-democratic government combined with a stable social environment and shared economic success.

As the United States moves increasingly to the left, despite the occasional temporary course corrections, we may find the United States with an equally unincentived population living off the historical successes of the country. Great technology and general mediocrity may be the rule for both China and the United States.

11. https://www.scmp.com/news/china/science/article/3296098/chinas-rd-growth-passes-us496-billion-steady-rise-hi-tech-dominance

4. Artificial Intelligence. Much as electrification accelerated value creation, AI will reshape value creation. "Omohundro [Institute] predicts self-aware, self-improving systems will develop four primary drives that are similar to human biological drives: efficiency, self-preservation, resource acquisition, and creativity."[12] The biggest short-term effect in 2025 will be applied AI for corporate productivity and efficiency improvement. Mid-term, augmented collective intelligence will combine humans, agents, and models to manage processes such as supply chain and manufacturing. Also mid-term AI-based advances in materials science will be very common, particularly as applied to medicine. Long-term AI will redefine science, medicine, and engineering, replacing labwork with digital processes using AI. Eventually in 10–20 years quantum computing will enable us to make real advances on complex social problems. We know today how to technically solve most environmental problems, but we will need quantum computing to resolve the social issues such as poverty.

   AI will replace human coding. Trust in AI will increase and we will realize that hallucinations are just evidence of growing pains in a new technology. In a rare case, I agree with OpenAI. *AI in America: OpenAI's Economic Blueprint* states, "We believe that building enough infrastructure is not just vital for ensuring that AI around the world is based on US rather than China-based technology—it's an unmissable opportunity to catalyze a reindustrialization of the US. Successful nations turn resources into competitive advantages. In the AI era, chips, data, energy and talent are the resources that will underpin continued US leadership."[13] Andi Gutmans, VP/GM Engineering, Databases at Google explains. "2025 is the year where dark data lights up. The majority of today's data sits in unstructured formats such as documents, images, videos, audio, and more. AI and improved data systems will enable businesses to easily process and analyze all of this unstructured data in ways that will completely transform their ability to reason

12. James Barrat, Our Final Invention: Artificial Intelligence and the End of the Human Era. https://www.goodreads.com/work/quotes/23906757
13. https://cdn.openai.com/global-affairs/ai-in-america-oai-economic-blueprint-20250113.pdf

about and leverage their enterprise-wide data."[14] Raghu Madabushi, Director National Grid Partners, points out the continued importance of energy to the future of AI. "As LLMs grow in size and complexity, energy consumption becomes the critical bottleneck to their scalability. The narrative for 2025 will shift from simply building bigger models to optimizing training and inference processes for energy efficiency, cost-effectiveness, and sustainability."[15] And Rashmi Misra, Chief AI Officer, Analog Devices, makes the telling point about the increase in edge computing to combine remote data capture and processing. "By this time next year I predict that we'll be using even more specialized edge-AI chips to enable tasks with much more power efficiency, speed, and overall better performance. We'll likely see resource-constrained devices at the edge running more sophisticated AI algorithms."[16]

These advances in AI paint the future, but some will see only the risk of another new technology proliferating. There is an increasing need to consider what David Krakauer at SFI calls "the regulation, control and prediction" in a dynamic, nonlinear system built on AI. As the natural and manmade systems are integrated even more by ACI style AI, the possibility for error theoretically increases. However, this path to increasingly integrate computation and tangible systems (adaption) has been under constant development since the 1960s. This development is now supported by the use of advanced modeling, such as digital twins, which I believe significantly reduces the risk and especially the likelihood of catastrophic disasters.

This short, admittedly optimistic, update shows me why I think AI is the greatest tool in human history since mathematics and the foundation for the Second Renaissance. And, really, we have only been exploring the real range of applied AI for about 10–15 years. So we have much opportunity ahead and my hope is that we eventually can apply AI and quantum computing to address social problems.

14. Quantum Computing: AI at Exponential Speed.
15. https://www.fastcompany.com/91254053/25-experts-predict-how-ai-will-change-business-and-life-in-2025
16. Ibid.

I see a social problem as the most concerning risk with AI. To use modern AI requires significant data management infrastructure and computation resources. We need to create the free resources for AI that I described in Chapter 8. Every citizen needs the choice of free access to AI resources and proper training beginning in elementary school. To be without AI will be akin to not having electricity, worse than not reading, and only increase the social tension.

15

Cross-Sector Collaboration: Breaking Down the Silos Between Government, Academia, and the Private Sector

"Scientific research is not merely a process of fitting new data into old models or into constellations of models comprising larger theories. New data often break the old models and theories. One cannot use the rules of chess to analyze a game of Go, nor can we use particle physics to understand genetics. Wittgenstein thought of games as the supreme metaphor for the specificity and context-dependence of formal thought: new possibilities need to be explained with new rules. And, we might add, in what 'language' are these new rules written—natural language, mathematics, computer code?"

—David C. Krakauer, The Complex World: An Introduction to the Foundations of Complexity Science

In the current environment, we have little or no chance to effectively achieve meaningful collaboration between government, academia, and corporates without a completely new and different approach. The uncertainty and complexity of modern life, technology, and computation has reached such levels that no single organization remains fully informed, if they ever were. The "rugged" individualism that built the United States needs to be replaced by an "ecosystem" approach. *An ecosystem is the collective bringing together of the relevant and necessary stakeholders and their resources to more effectively, holistically and sustainably solve problems in a timely fashion at scale.*

Complexity economics provides some insight, as Bryan Arthur explains it.

> Complexity economics is basically seeing the economy not as a machine, balanced and perfect and humming along, but as an ecology. New strategies, new things are coming and going and striving to survive and do well in a situation they mutually create. We can describe this algorithmically, but not easily by equations, not just because the situation is complicated to track but because new behaviors and categories of behavior are not easily captured by equations.[1]

Effectively we need to set aside what we have been taught for thousands of years, reject a top-down hierarchical model and embrace the fluidity of modern, high tech, networked work and life. Systems thinking complements complexity science and gives us much guidance on a new approach. Leyla Acaraglu, an early MIT researcher in the field of systems thinking explains.

> Systems thinking is about understanding how things connect together; it requires a broader perspective than just the isolated aspects of your own product, service, or business. In the context of circular economy activation, it's a foundation for framing the product as part of the system it exists within, such as the supply chain, consumer value and ecosystem requirements.[2]

This is the model best suited to modern multi-party collaboration to address complex sociocultural, technological, economic, and environmental problems. Complexity and systems thinking reinforce each other to support the nested hierarchies, adaptive models, and networked systems that can only be truly understood with the mathematics of graph theory. More simply, such

1. W. Brian Arthur, Eric D. Beinhocker, and Allison Stanger. *Complexity Economics.*
2. https://www.linkedin.com/pulse/6-principles-circular-economy-leyla-acaroglu-hxnxe/

systems are the self-directed systems that provide the necessary adaptability to deal with modern life and multiple stakeholders in real time.

Mr. S. Rajaratnam, Singapore's Minister for Foreign Affairs (1979), explained the point well.

> There are the practical men who maintain that such speculations are a waste of time and they have no bearing at all on solutions to immediate day-to-day problems. This may have been so in earlier periods of history when changes were few and minute and were spread over decades and centuries... Because we are not only living in a world of accelerating change but also of changes which are global in scope and which permeate almost all aspects of human activity... Since change is about the future then only a future-oriented society can cope with the problems of the 21st century.[3]

The Minister makes clear what the U.S. government, corporations, and academia must do. The siloed approach that served the United States well since its founding is now out of date, incapable of analyzing, planning, and executing to achieve tangible solutions at scale. The trend in the United States is not encouraging, with few organizations proposing workable solutions and few efforts forthcoming to create multi-stakeholder ecosystems to effectively solve problems. Maybe we need a Martin Luther King, a heroic, self-directed leader to build a new consensus and plans, but I cannot think of any figure in the United States to play such a role. Perhaps that is why the new tools have appeared, as Bryan Arthur would predict, and we have agentic models and ACI.

Agentic AI is a system designed to operate autonomously using multiple ML agents, adapt to dynamic environments, and achieve specific goals. These systems act independently and purposefully without constant human intervention.[4] In simple terms, ACI integrates the human to synergistically complement the AI systems and take responsibility for decision-making and the outcome. Increasingly, I see the federal government

3. https://file.go.gov.sg/csfforesight2024.pdf
4. https://www.ibm.com/think/topics/agentic-ai

more and more as simply a participant and less as the leader. As problems are increasingly managed in accordance with CAS teachings, solutions will be envisioned as bottom up hierarchical approaches and in this model a city or county government might take the lead. The NSF Regional Innovations Engines program and the EDA Regional Technology and Innovation Hub Program both explicitly endorse such a "local" approach to social and economic problem-solving and development, with the federal government in large part merely providing the funding and the typical periodic reviews required by law. The federal agencies also award the funding to a local project lead such as a university or city. However, not to be misleading, I have great respect for the NSF and I quote their description of the Engines program to make clear the *objectives* of their funding and the local objectives.

> The U.S. National Science Foundation Regional Innovation Engines (NSF Engines) program was established to advance transdisciplinary, collaborative, use-inspired and translational research and technology development in key technology focus areas.
>
> Each NSF Engine can receive **up to $160 million** to support the development of regional coalitions of researchers, institutions and companies to conduct research and development that engages people in the process of creating solutions with economic and societal impacts. Through the process, NSF Engines will train and develop the local workforce and grow regional innovation ecosystems throughout the U.S.

Cities, counties, and states would do well to remember the NSF objective of transdisciplinary research and the need for related technology development. Such research is the highest possible standard and objective in research.

Note: One counter example may be OpenAI. With respect to "coordinating and collaborating" with the federal government, OpenAI recommends "form a consortium that identifies best practices for working with the national security community, including to prioritize security-based requests of the government (such as access to compute) and to streamline efforts to responsibly integrate AI in ways consistent with US and company policies."[5]

5. https://cdn.openai.com/global-affairs/ai-in-america-oai-economic-blueprint-20250113.pdf

16

Ethics and Innovation: Navigating the Moral Landscape

> "'Act now, at speed, and at scale' is the prudent response. This holds true not only for pandemics, but for the climate risk and other systemic tail risks."[1]
>
> —NIH

I find much of the current discussion on ethics to be very shallow and naive, bastardized to critique an activity or technology such as AI. Metaethics is a normative pursuit to understand the foundations of morality and to describe rather than prescribe. Values shape morality but can evolve over time. The American values today remain little changed since the founding of the country, with the exception of a more explicit statement against discrimination based on sex, race, and culture. Those values are:

1. Individual Freedom and Privacy
2. Self-reliance
3. A strong Work Ethic
4. Democracy and Justice
5. Optimism and Progress.

1. https://pmc.ncbi.nlm.nih.gov/articles/PMC7533687/

Many people opine on this subject of values. I will acknowledge USAHello[2] who describe themselves as "an online center for information and education for refugees, asylum seekers, immigrants and welcoming communities." With "my" values declared, I can now look to understand the ethical issues that shape my new approach to governance, which are shown below.

- AI
- Cross-sector collaboration
- Reduced federal government.

I choose to start with AI given the frequency of people's concerns about ethical issues.

ARTIFICIAL INTELLIGENCE

If we look at individual freedom, I think AI provides superlative, low-cost world-class tools to anybody with network connectivity. Such tools should breakdown barriers that can hold back individual initiative. Privacy in AI is a hot topic. Personally I have assumed since the early 1980s, and the first networked computers, that all my digital voice, data, and text is monitored by the federal government and increasingly also by the Chinese government. Therefore, I am desensitized to the privacy concern. Simply use the grandmother rule. Do nothing you would not tell your grandmother. And always remember, if your privacy standards are not met by the U.S. government or industry, move to another country. Europe is well on the way to crushing individual initiative and entrepreneurship with enhanced privacy regulations based on concerns about AI. A last thought on privacy. Why have we not publicly debated privacy issues related to Google Search. For almost thirty years, Google has captured every search by every individual user, but I recall little public concern. Could it be that bad actors are active now and trying to undermine democracy in the United States … and perhaps even trying to set the entire social agenda. *The social agenda has an important place in democracy, but I merely wish to point out how easy it is*

2. https://usahello.org/life-in-usa/culture/american-values/

today for bad actors to shape it. Hedge fund operator and now author Ray Dalio believes that internal social division is one of the three conditions to signal a declining empire.

OpenAI makes the important points well in their "AI in America: OpenAI's Economic Blueprint." "Rules and regulations for the development and use of AI should be based on the democratic values the country has always stood for—what we think of as 'democratic AI' … The US strategy … should prioritize national competitiveness, model safeguards and national security."[3] Model safeguards!! Universities such as Carnegie Mellon research and write on the current state of model safeguards in a very even handed and objective way.

CROSS-SECTOR COLLABORATION

Indigenous people and native populations have always organized in a way consistent with CAS. They preserve the individual and their rights, encourage self-organizing in their more simple approach to life, limit top-down hierarchy, and support adaptive behavior. It is only in the last 200–300 years that man has really moved away from man's earliest behaviors, the simplicity of local communities, and enhanced engagement.

If we look back to understand top-down hierarchy and the model of federal government, we must trace information and its flow. Top-down hierarchies typically exist to control information and related opportunity or to serve as the lowest cost repository for reliable information. We can debate which logic explains the United States. Regardless, today we have widespread, low-cost, networked sources of reliable information and the need for any government to serve as a central repository is nearly nonexistent. A temporary storage for anonymized health data might be a temporary need, hopefully soon to be replaced by private companies incentivized for purposes we may not yet imagine or appreciate.

3. https://cdn.openai.com/global-affairs/ai-in-america-oai-economic-blueprint-20250113.pdf

If we are optimistic about the future and the progress to be made, one behavior will be critical. Multidisciplinary approaches will become common and interdisciplinary approaches the standard of excellence. Modern complexity requires such an approach and the NSF is a prominent advocate for multidisciplinarity. Such cross-sector collaboration will require retraining of academic faculty who frequently use siloed approaches. Not to single out academics, much of my proposal for reduced federal government services will also require retraining of staff on interdisciplinary approaches.

REDUCED FEDERAL GOVERNMENT

With the advances in AI, I hope to see the federal and subnational governments all use AI more. The objectives should be better citizen services—to repeat, better citizen services—and lower cost, faster, easy-to-use government interaction. Such an approach should make most of government administrative services a behind the scenes, unobtrusive experience. Perhaps someday all government administrative interactions will be done by AI agentic models on both sides of the inquiry or issue. As McAfee and Brynjolfsson state, "But the overall pattern is clear: in case after case, when a model can be created and tested, it tends to perform as well as, or better than, human experts making similar decisions. Too often, we continue to rely on human judgment when machines can do better."[4] In a more inspirational view, former HBS professor Pierre Wack tells us, "to design scenarios that would lead our decision makers to question their inner model of reality and change it as necessary, in order to take action."[5] We need for the leaders and the citizens of the United States to "question their models" and design, develop, and update their twenty-first century model of the democratic federal government. We have the tools today, provided by AI, but can we act in time to avoid …

4. Machine, Platform, Crowd: Harnessing Our Digital Future …

5. Wack, Pierre. 1984. *Scenarios: The Gentle Art of Re-perceiving.* Boston: Harvard Business School.

17

Conclusions

> "Most important, I recognized for the first time that to see AI as a science unto itself was to miss its greatest potential. Our research was demonstrating that, when integrated with other fields, and pushed by other forms of expertise, AI's possibilities might be limitless."
>
> —Fei-Fei Li, The Worlds I See.

The future will be shaped by artificial intelligence, complexity science, and entrepreneurship; the risks to undermine that strategy are environmental collapse and U.S. and Chinese governments' political ambitions. Applied AI is the future of science, technology, and the social system. Man's survival will be shaped by the complexity science that explains both natural and manmade systems and their interactions. Mike Maples, one of my favorite writers on contemporary themes, makes the point forcefully.

> Now, more than ever, the world needs more entrepreneurs, who have the courage to step up, in the face of great odds and design an exponentially different future. The present has stopped working. We must create a different future.[1]

1. https://medium.com/@m2jr/how-to-build-a-breakthrough-3071b6415b06

The NSF validates this thinking when it recommends that every graduate student must learn AI, multidisciplinary approaches, and entrepreneurship, regardless of their field of study or postgraduate plans. Private entrepreneurship, individual initiative, and capital should shape the future. If we are going to rely on government, Washington must focus on the environment, energy, defense, and research in science, engineering, and medicine. Subnational government must step up to improve the quality of education and healthcare. In all of this, David Krakauer, President of SFI, explains the role of complexity science well.

> The application of complexity scholarship to global commons problems, including disease, climate, conflict, and political economy, is likely to be an essential component in any effort to ensure the prosperity and survival of life on Earth … The integrated nature of complexity science aligns with the connected nature of the modern world. Complexity science will be essential to all future projects that aim to escape terminal planetary decline.[2]

Italian professor Roberto Poli offers a theory of the future that includes "predictions, discoveries, and anticipations."[3] I conclude here with remarks on each of the three topics.

PREDICTIONS

Predictions are techniques such as forecasts, trend analysis, and modeling.

Although renewable energy surpassed coal fired generation in 2022 and nuclear generation in 2020, I am doubtful that the United States, and equally important the world, can reach the UN Net Zero Coalition goals for 2050. Most importantly, the six largest emitters of greenhouse gases (63%)—China, India, the EU, the Russian Federation, Brazil, and the Unit-

2. https://santafe.edu/news-center/news/sfi-press-announces-the-complex-world
3. https://www.egeaeditore.it/ita/prodotti/societa-e-cultura/lavorare-con-il-futuro.aspx

ed States—must aggressively focus on the target to halt global increase in temperature to 1.5°C compared with pre-industrial levels.[4] I am extremely doubtful about reaching this target, but if I had another 60+ years to live, I would devote my life to entrepreneurial solutions to this problem. Human colonies on Mars or even the moon would not be my strategy. Replacing all CO_2 emissions from energy through 100% renewable energy sources would probably be where I would focus.

On healthcare I am much more upbeat. AI is the perfect tool to produce personal and scalable solutions to health issues, given the nature of the fundamental components of chemistry and biology and their suitability to manipulation by AI. If we can apply AI to speed up and reduce the cost of new pharmaceutical approvals, that further accelerates the improvement and cost reduction of healthcare. Another promising field is the application of AI to treating psychological and psychiatric disorders. AI for prediction, diagnosis, treatment, and support are all active fields. I mentored an NIH-funded team for three years using ML to support distressed children of abusive parents. The platform offered multiple treatment options based on research findings by multiple doctors in real time.

I teach an undergraduate course called "Living forever." It is a combination of modern science, medicine, and life planning for what I think will likely be a student life of 100–120 years. Most of us have no life plan or copy our parents. Few have a plan for life of 100+ years supported by science and medicine advanced by applied AI. I am hoping for 90–100 years and I would like to thank my Medtronics pacemaker for making every day possible.

Predicting the future of education is much more challenging, not to develop the solutions but rather to shape a consensus. Everyone has gone to school, which makes them think they are an expert on education. I have been in education since 2009, I was schooled in the teachings of Jean Piaget working on an educational project at the MIT Media Lab. I see the self-directed initiative of my Honors College students at FIU every day to shape their future through learning. I think education will become intentionally

4.

multidisciplinary, probably encouraged by more curriculum based on applied AI. I think that science education will become more important because of the opportunities that AI will make possible and the challenge from the Chinese to take the lead in multiple technologies. I would like to see more remote digital instruction to introduce learning material, more AI-assisted bot learning and teachers focused to help with the Q&A to validate learning. Teachers' unions will feel threatened by anything similar to my approach and the teachers themselves may feel the same. Vision is disruptive. Alpha Schools and similar concepts are coming!! Self-directed, active learning should be the model for the future.

The future of defense really comes down to one's view of the Chinese strategy. Ukraine has taught us a lot about the current state of warfare, the technologies that work, and the opportunities for military technological advantage. If I were the Chinese, I would wait us out, not invade Taiwan but stress us into increased military expenditures. Eventually the United States becomes like Brazil … unstable, bankrupt with no will power to change or … fight. This scenario may not come to pass. The findings of the Trump administration may uncover so much government misspending and corruption that Americans on the left may be ready for a change to fiscal responsibility. The greater likelihood is that the population of China becomes so disenfranchised with Yi Jinping's strategy that China needs a war "caused by the Americans" to distract the population from their misery. Such a scenario will likely take years to develop, if it ever does.

DISCOVERIES

Unanticipated phenomena or insights based in theoretical frameworks are discoveries. By 2050, I expect the following advances …

1. Investopedia defines quantum computing simply as a field of computer science that leverages the principles of quantum mechanics to process information. Unlike classical computers, which use bits (0 or

1) to encode data, quantum computers use qubits, which can exist in multiple states simultaneously due to phenomena like superposition and entanglement. This allows quantum computers to perform complex calculations exponentially faster than classical systems for specific problems.[5] Hartmut Neven, Google's VP of Engineering, anticipates this technology may be commercialized within five years. While it will be used to improve AI, modeling, and cybersecurity, my hope is that it is applied to develop computation-based solutions to social problems.

2. Small Modular Reactors (SMRs) are advanced nuclear fission reactors with a capacity of ~300 MW. These reactors have production capacity of about one-third of a traditional reactor. Such plants are expected to be operational in the mid-2030s and supply large data centers, communities, and desalinization projects.
3. Nuclear fusion is a process in which two or more light atomic nuclei combine to form a heavier nucleus, releasing a significant amount of energy. The sun is an example of such an energy system. The technology may be ready for commercialization after 2030. Assuming successful advances in research, it would be the most economical and reliable source of large-scale energy. I believe that the risks should prove to be acceptable.
4. Precision Medicine is AI-enabled personalized treatments by integrating genetic, proteomic, and clinical data, streamlining complex processes that traditionally relied on artisanal approaches. AI plays a transformative role in personalized medicine by enabling the analysis of complex, multi-dimensional data to create individually tailored healthcare strategies. Precision oncology is the most advanced segment. Applications of this technology are forecast by *Research Nester* to reach US$757.4B by 2037.[6]

5. https://www.investopedia.com/terms/q/quantum-computing.asp
6. https://www.researchnester.com/reports/precision-medicine-market/6315

ANTICIPATIONS

Anticipation involves using past and present information to model and prepare for future scenarios that frequently involve emergent behavior.

I see Nassim Taleb's "black swans," as described in *The Black Swan* and *Antifragile*, as "anticipated" events. Uncertain and unpredictable events, such as energy blackouts, pandemics, earthquakes, Force 6 hurricanes, and mass wildfires are examples. Most commentators anticipate an increase in the frequency and scale of such events. Energy blackouts and maybe pandemics are "manmade." All the other events demonstrate the effects of exploiting the environment.

A CLOSING THOUGHT

As we increasingly adopt new applications of AI, we are likely to become overly reliant on computation as a source of solutions. These technological advances will tend to move us away from the conceptual innovations that may be our salvation. More important than the pace of adoption of AI or quantum computing, we need to redefine democratic government in the United States, modernize education, and accelerate remediation of the environment.

The United States is the last bastion of democracy for the planet. No other democratic country has the resources and will power to face up to the increasing threat from China, the increasing list of U.S. enemy countries and the state-sponsored bad actors. We need to modernize democracy in the United States to take on this challenge and many more.

www.ingramcontent.com/pod-product-compliance
Lightning Source LLC
LaVergne TN
LVHW022053200926
848481LV00003B/887
* 9 7 9 8 3 8 5 1 8 1 6 2 9 *